12759

EYES
&
SEEING

Books by Joan Elma Rahn

SEEING WHAT PLANTS DO

HOW PLANTS TRAVEL

GROCERY STORE BOTANY

MORE ABOUT WHAT PLANTS DO

HOW PLANTS ARE POLLINATED

THE METRIC SYSTEM

ALFALFA, BEANS & CLOVER

GROCERY STORE ZOOLOGY

SEVEN WAYS TO COLLECT PLANTS

WATCH IT GROW, WATCH IT CHANGE

TRAPS AND LURES IN THE LIVING WORLD

EYES AND SEEING

EYES
&
SEEING

Joan Elma Rahn

with illustrations by the author

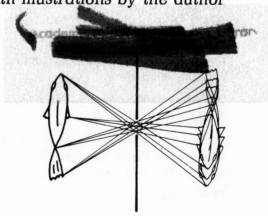

ATHENEUM   New York   1981

Library of Congress Cataloging in Publication Data

Rahn, Joan Elma, date
  Eyes and seeing.

  Bibliography: p. 106
  Includes index.
  SUMMARY: Describes some diverse types of eyes from
flatworms to humans. Includes information on light and simple
experiments.
    1. Eye—Juvenile literature. 2. Vision—Juvenile
literature. [1. Eye. 2. Vision] I. Title.
QP475.7.R33   591.1'823   80-23988
ISBN 0-689-30828-0

Published simultaneously in Canada by
McClelland & Stewart, Ltd.

Manufactured by R.R. Donnelley & Sons, Inc.
Composed by Dix Typesetting Co. Inc.
Designed by Maria Epes

First Edition

Contents

CHAPTER 1 / Light and Vision 3

CHAPTER 2 / An Ocellus and a Pinhole Eye 8

CHAPTER 3 / Something Better than a Pinhole:

A Lens 16

CHAPTER 4 / The Human Eye 22

CHAPTER 5 / The Retina 33

CHAPTER 6 / Adapting to Light and Dark 51

CHAPTER 7 / Seeing More or Seeing Better 67

CHAPTER 8 / Insect Eyes 83

CHAPTER 9 / Seeing with Mirrors 98

More About Eyes 106

Glossary 109

Index 115

EYES
&
SEEING

CHAPTER 1 / *Light and Vision*

MOST OF THIS BOOK is about eyes and seeing. What is necessary for vision? Several things: light, an eye that contains certain pigments called *visual pigments,* and a brain that is stimulated when these pigments absorb light. The visual pigments are confined to certain cells within the eye called *photoreceptors,* a term that means "receivers of light."

But before we can talk about vision, we need to say something about light. In everyday conversations we say that we see light, and although we cannot see without it, we actually do not see the light itself as it passes through the air. Imagine a room with one window. If rays of sunlight came through the window, and if we could see the light itself, it would block out our view of anything behind it (Fig. 1).

When the light hits an object in the room, the wall, for instance, the light is reflected away at various angles—toward the ceiling and the floor, let us say. If we could see that reflected light as well, even more of the room would be blocked out. In fact, because light is reflected from the many surfaces of all the objects in the room, if we could actually see light, we probably would never see any of the objects, for the air is "filled" with light rays whenever it is not dark. The room would appear as just a mass of bright light.

We see objects because light from some source, such as the sun or a lamp, strikes the objects and then is reflected into our eyes. Only the light that actually reaches the photoreceptors in our eyes enables us to see an object. We see a tree when light from the sun strikes the tree and some of it is reflected into our eyes (Fig. 2). Light that strikes the tree and is reflected elsewhere contributes nothing to our vision.

In a dusty room you sometimes see what appears to be a beam of sunlight entering a window—much like the sunbeam in the middle of Figure 1. Again, what you are seeing is not light itself, but thousands of tiny dust particles in the

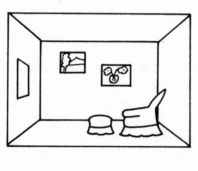

A room as we see it.

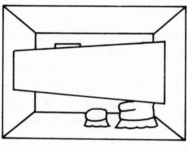

A room as we would see it if we actually saw a beam of light as it entered a room.

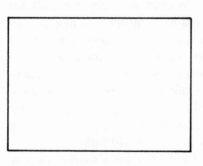

A room as we would see it if we saw all the light reflected back and forth within the room.

Fig. 1. *We cannot see light itself.*

air. Each reflects some light toward your eye. Because they are small, you usually don't notice each particle individually; but if the air is thick with dust, together they give the impression of a "solid" sunbeam.

If we cannot see light, what then do we mean by visible light? And how does it differ from invisible light? Light is one part of a vast spectrum of electromagnetic radiation all of which is described as traveling in waves—something like the waves of water in a lake or pond. However, you cannot see waves of light for at least two reasons. First of all, since you cannot see light itself, you could hardly see its waves. And second, the waves themselves are much too small to be seen, even if you could see light (Fig. 3). They are so small they are measured in nanometers. (A nanometer is one billionth of a meter.)

Light of different wavelengths appears to us to be of different colors. When sufficient electromagnetic radiation with wavelengths of about 380 to 430 nanometers enters the eye and is absorbed by the visual pigments in the photore-

Fig. 2. *The tree is visible to the boy because of the rays of sunlight that are reflected from the tree and reach his eye. Rays of light that are reflected elsewhere have nothing to do with his vision.*

ceptors, we have the impression of seeing violet; if the wave-length is about 430 to 470 nanometers, we have the impression of seing blue, and so on. These and some other wavelengths are shown in Figure 4.

What we call light is the electromagnetic radiation of wavelengths of about 380 to 760 nanometers; these are the lengths that when they enter our eyes are absorbed by visual pigments. This is the light we call *visible light*. Visible light includes the colors we see in a rainbow—violet, blue, blue-green, green, yellow, orange, and red. Sunlight includes all of them and is called white light because a mixture of all these colors appears white to us. Visible light is the light we ordinarily say we *see*, although what we really mean is that it is the light we *see something else by*.

Even though we speak of white light or red light or violet light, as you might suspect from what has just been

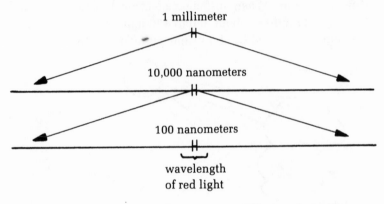

1 millimeter

10,000 nanometers

100 nanometers

wavelength
of red light

Fig. 3. *The short upper line is one millimeter long. The middle line shows the millimeter enlarged to 100 times its length. The short area marked off in the center of this line represents 10,000 nanometers (magnified 100 times). In real life you cannot see anything as small as 10,000 nanometers without using a microscope or a strong magnifying glass. The bottom line shows this small area magnified another 100 times (total magnification 10,000 times). The short area marked off in the center of this line represents 100 nanometers. The bracket indicates the longest wavelengths of red light.*

said, light itself is not colored. Depending on what wavelength or combination of wavelengths of light reach the visual pigments in the eye, we receive the impression of one or more colors. We see green grass because grass reflects light of wavelengths of about 500 to 560 nanometers, and this light enters our eyes and stimulates certain photoreceptors there. We see a red tomato because the tomato reflects light of wavelengths of about 650 to 760 nanometers, and this light stimulates other photoreceptors.

Invisible light (also called *black light*) is electromagnetic radiation of wavelengths shorter than 380 nanometers (ultraviolet) or longer than 760 nanometers (infrared). They are called invisible because we ordinarily cannot see by them—either because they do not reach the photoreceptors in the eye, or, if they do, because they do not stimulate the photoreceptors. A room illuminated with only ultraviolet light, for instance, would look totally black to us.

Some animals can see by at least some wavelengths of light invisible to us, and they may not be able to see by some wavelengths visible to us. Bees, for instance, can see by ultraviolet light but not by red light. If bees were writing this book, they would say that visible light ranges from ultraviolet to orange, and not from violet to red, as we do.

What we and other animals see, then, depends in part on the light that enters the eye. It also depends on the structure of the eye itself, and that is what most of the rest of this book is about.

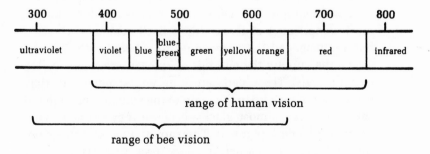

Fig. 4. *The spectrum of light visible to human beings and bees. Wavelengths are given in nanometers.*

CHAPTER 2 / An Ocellus and a Pinhole Eye

AMONG THE MOST ELEMENTARY KINDS of eyes found in living creatures are the ocellus and the pinhole eye. The word *ocellus* means "little eye." Several invertebrate animals (animals without backbones) have ocelli rather than the more complicated seeing equipment we normally think of as eyes. Among them are some flatworms, jellyfishes, starfishes, and insects. The simplest ocelli have no lenses and do not focus light into images as our own eyes do. In this chapter we will consider an ocellus without a lens—as well as the pinhole eye, which also lacks a lens. Chapter 8 includes a description of some insect ocelli, which do have lenses and may form crude images.

Dugesia (also called *Planaria*) is a flatworm studied in many biology laboratories. This animal has two ocelli. They are not the simplest of ocelli in the animal kingdom, nor the most complicated of them either. Each ocellus of *Dugesia* has a cup-shaped tissue made up of *pigment cells* (Fig. 5). Inside the cup are the endings of special nerve cells called *retinula cells*. These cells are long and slender, and they extend out of the cup to the brain of the animal. The pigment cells are dark—almost black—because they contain many granules of a dark pigment. This cup of pigment cells is not the photoreceptor. Rather, the dark tissue protects the retinula cells from light that comes from all directions but one, the direction in which the opening of the cup is pointed.

It is the retinula cells that are the photoreceptors—or, more specifically, just their enlarged tips, called *retinula clubs*, which lie within the cup. These are the cells that are sensitive to light, and although they look quite pale, the retinula clubs are believed to contain a small amount of visual pigment. Light striking a retinula club is absorbed by the visual pigment, and this starts a nervous impulse that travels the length of the entire retinula cell and then reaches the brain.

Dugesia, with only two ocelli and no true eyes, cannot see actual objects as we do. That is, the animal cannot see forms and shapes. It can see only light, and can distinguish light from dark. To get a rough idea of what the world looks like through such an ocellus, take two layers of waxed paper and hold them before your eyes, making sure that the paper curves around the side of your head so that you can't see around the edges. The waxed paper will distort the light

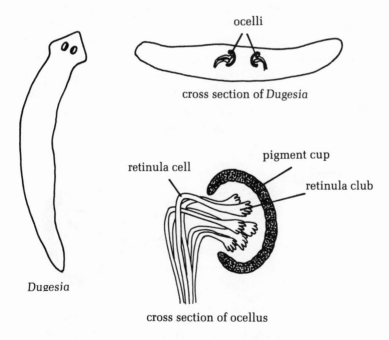

ocelli

cross section of *Dugesia*

retinula cell

pigment cup

retinula club

Dugesia

cross section of ocellus

Fig. 5.   DUGESIA (PLANARIA) *has two simple eyes.*

rays enough that you won't be able to distinguish much more than light and dark areas. You will be able to see that it is light near the window or a lamp and darker in some other parts of the room, but you won't be able to see the actual shape of the window or the lamp.

The arrangement of the pigment cups, which gives *Dugesia* a rather cross-eyed appearance, helps the animal to determine direction of light and darkness. If *Dugesia* is illuminated only from the right, then retinula cells in the right ocellus receive a great deal of light, but the retinula cells in the left ocellus, being shaded by their pigment cup, receive very little light. Then the brain receives many nervous impulses from the right ocellus, and very few from the left. The animal becomes aware of where bright light and shadows are, and this determines the direction in which it moves. If more light comes from the right, the animal moves to the left, for *Dugesia* is an animal that feeds on decaying matter among the fallen leaves and other debris on the bottoms of streams. These are usually dark areas, and *Dugesia* nearly always moves away from light and toward darkness. Being able to tell light from dark seems to be all the vision this animal needs.

To get an idea of what things look like to *Dugesia* with its two ocelli pointed in different directions, hold the double layer of waxed paper before your eyes again. Then, because your eyes do not point in opposite directions as those of

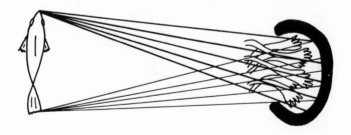

Fig. 6. *The simple eye of* DUGESIA *is sensitive to light but does not focus it. Each retinula cell receives light from all parts of the object(s) before it.*

Dugesia do, hold a piece of cardboard or a small box about three or four inches wide directly against your nose. This will block your view directly ahead and will separate what you see into right and left patches of light. This must be approximately what *Dugesia* sees.

The reason *Dugesia* cannot see forms and shapes is that its ocelli do not focus light rays on the photoreceptors. In Figure 6, light rays reflected from the head of the fish enter the wide opening of the ocellus at several angles, and together they strike all the photoreceptive retinula clubs. So do all the light rays from the tail. This illustration shows only the light rays reflected from two points on the fish, but you can easily imagine what it would look like if similar rays had been drawn from every point on the fish. There would be light rays from every part of the fish striking every retinula club. When this happens, no image is formed, for every retinula club "sees" every part of the fish.

An image can be focused in an eye only when each photoreceptor receives light from a different part of the object being viewed. There are three ways that eyes focus light —one is with a pinhole, one is with a lens, and one is with a mirror. Nearly all true eyes focus light with lenses, and a few do it with mirrors. Only one animal, the *Nautilus*, has eyes that focus with a pinhole.

The *Nautilus* eye blocks out all light rays except the few that come through a small pinhole opening (Fig. 7). Opposite the pinhole is the *retina*, which is a tissue of photoreceptor cells. Because light travels in straight lines, light rays from one part of the fish strike only one part of the retina, and each part of the retina receives light rays from only one part of the fish. To put it another way, an image of the fish has been focused on the retina of the *Nautilus* eye. When this happens, the cells of the optic nerve transmit stimuli to the brain, which is what actually identifies the image of the fish. *Dugesia* would have had only the impression of light, then dark, then light if the fish had passed near one of its ocelli.

Notice that the retinal image of the fish in the *Nautilus* eye is upside down with reference to the fish itself. One of the functions of the brain is to interpret this image as right side up. Then the animal sees the fish as it actually is.

To demonstrate that a pinhole really focuses light, obtain a piece of waxed paper, a rather sturdy needle (like a darning needle), a fairly large piece of cardboard, and a lamp. The cardboard ought not to be corrugated cardboard; the kind that comes on the backs of writing pads or typing paper is a good thickness and size. It would be best if the lamp is the type that throws light in only one direction. A candle would be even better, but you may not want to work with a burning candle for safety reasons.

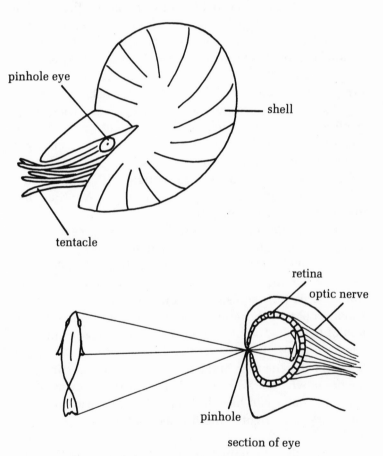

Fig. 7. The NAUTILUS has a pinhole eye.

With the needle, poke a hole near the center of the cardboard and, if necessary, wiggle the needle around a bit so that the hole is about 1 millimeter across. At night, when it is dark, light the lamp. Turn off other lights in the room and close any doors and draw any shades or curtains to keep all other light out. Now stand about 5 to 10 feet away from the lamp. With one hand hold the cardboard at arm's length so that the pinhole is directly between the lamp and your eyes. With the other hand, hold the waxed paper about half way between the cardboard and your eyes (Fig. 8). The waxed paper will serve as a screen on which the image focused by the pinhole will appear. In this demonstration, the waxed paper represents the retina of the *Nautilus* eye.

If you move the waxed paper farther away from the pinhole, the image will become larger, but it will also become fainter because the same amount of light is coming through the pinhole, but it is now spread over a larger area. If you move the waxed paper closer to the pinhole, the image will become smaller and brighter—now because the same amount of light is spread over a smaller area. Except when the waxed paper is very close to the cardboard—touching it or nearly so—the image is always in focus no matter what

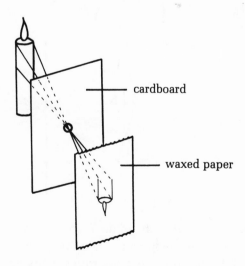

cardboard

waxed paper

Fig. 8. *How to demonstrate focusing with a pinhole.*

the distance between the waxed paper and the pinhole. You can also move the cardboard closer to or farther from the light, and the image will still be in focus.

This feature of always remaining in focus is probably the only advantageous feature of the pinhole image. The *Nautilus* eye does not have to make any adjustments—as nearly all eyes with lenses must—when the object being viewed moves nearer or farther away, for the object always stays in focus.

Despite this, there is a big disadvantage to the pinhole: it lets very little light into the eye, and so very little strikes the retina. Unless the object being viewed through the pinhole is a very bright one, the image is rather dim, and a dim image cannot be seen as well as a bright one.

The image would be brighter if the pinhole were larger,

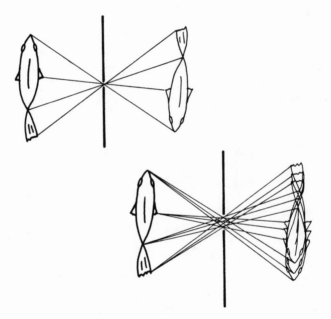

Fig. 9. *The smaller the pinhole, the sharper the focus. A large hole allows so many light rays from each point to enter that it has the effect of forming many overlapping images that confuse the eye.*

but this would cause a new problem. About four inches away from the pinhole in your cardboard put another, larger hole—one that has a diameter about twice as large as the diameter of the first hole. Hold this second, larger pinhole between the lamp and the waxed paper. The image will be brighter, but it will also appear to be less sharp. You can see why this is so if you imagine the larger hole to be made up of several small ones. If each one forms a separate image, and if the images are in slightly different places but mostly overlap each other, you probably will still be able to tell what the object is, but the image will be blurred (Fig. 9).

The larger the hole, the brighter and more blurred the image will be. A large hole produces such a fuzzy image that there really is no image at all, and the hole is useless for focusing. In fact, if you make a hole in the cardboard large enough to do this, you will have a representation of the ocellus of *Dugesia*, which has a very large opening that does not focus an image.

The *Dugesia* ocellus, then, allows a bright blur of light to reach its photoreceptors, and the *Nautilus* pinhole forms a sharp but rather dim image. Is there a way to form a bright, sharp image? Yes, and that way is with an eye that has a large opening and a lens.

CHAPTER 3 / Something Better than a Pinhole: A Lens

LENSES ARE SPECIALLY SHAPED pieces of transparent material. Most commercial lenses are made from glass or plastic. In the eyes of living things, lenses are usually composed of living, transparent cells.

A lens bends light rays. The pinhole that we considered in Chapter 2 did not bend light rays; the rays passed through in a straight line. The pinhole focused light only because the light entered through a tiny opening. A lens, on the other hand, permits light to pass through a larger area, and the lens focuses light rays by bending them.

Light rays always travel in straight lines unless something causes them to bend. One type of bending of light is called *refraction*. Refraction occurs when light passes from one transparent substance to another. The degree of bending depends on the nature of the two substances and the angle at which light strikes the interface (their common boundary) where they meet. Let us suppose, for example, that light passes through air, a thick pane of glass, and then air again. If the light strikes the interface at 90° (perpendicular to the surfaces), the light passing through these three would not be refracted. The light ray will pass straight through without being bent. Anyone using this ray to view an object will see the object exactly where it is (Fig. 10).

But if light strikes the air-glass interface at some other angle, the light ray will be bent in such a way as to become more nearly perpendicular to the interface. Then the light travels through the glass in a new straight line until it reaches the glass-air interface. Here it bends again, and this time it bends away from the perpendicular. In the case of a flat piece of glass with its two sides parallel to each other, the line made by light ray emerging from the glass is parallel to the line made by the light ray before it entered the glass. Anyone viewing an object by this ray will see the object where it is not; it will appear to be somewhat to the side of its true position.

With glass of a given thickness, the more acute the angle

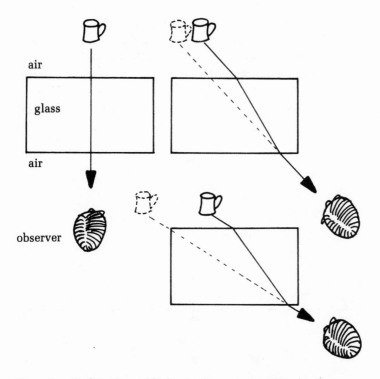

Fig. 10. *Refraction of light. Light rays usually are bent when they pass from air to glass and from glass to air. This makes an object appear to be where it actually is not. Only if light strikes the interface perpendicularly (left) does it move on without being bent.*

at which the original light ray strikes the glass, the more it is refracted, and the more an object on the other side of the glass seems to be displaced.

In addition, the thicker the glass, the more the object seems to be displaced even though the angle of refraction remains the same. If a pane of glass is very thin, the apparent displacement of the object will be barely noticeable.

The flat piece of glass we have been talking about does not focus an image. As many rays of light come from the object, each strikes the glass at a different angle and eventually is refracted to a different place (Fig. 11). But if a piece of glass is cut to such a shape that all the light rays reaching it from a single point on an object are refracted to meet again at another point on the other side of the glass, then those light rays are in focus where they meet. If light rays from each point on the object can be similarly focused, each at its own appropriate spot on the other side of the glass, then an image is in focus. A piece of glass that does this is a lens.

In Figure 12, three rays of light are shown radiating from each of two points on a fish. Because the two surfaces

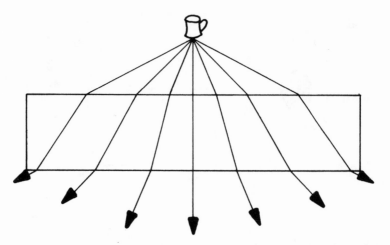

Fig. 11. *A flat piece of glass does not focus light. That is, the rays of light radiating from one point (on the cup) are not all brought back to one point on the other side of the glass.*

of the lens are not parallel to each other, when a light ray emerges from the lens its course is not necessarily parallel to the course it took before entering the lens. It is true, as before, however, that after entering the lens, the light ray becomes more nearly perpendicular to the surface (remember it is a curved surface here), and that after leaving the lens, the light ray is farther from the perpendicular than it was in the lens (again, it has passed through another curved surface). It is because of the curved surfaces that the light rays that came from a certain point on an object meet again on the other side of the lens and form an image. Of course, the lens must be properly shaped to do this; not just any shape will do.

If a piece of paper is placed where the image forms, the image may be visible on the paper. To perform your own demonstration of this, all you need is the lamp and the waxed paper that you used before and an ordinary magnifying glass, which is a glass or plastic lens. Again, light the lamp in an otherwise darkened room. Hold the paper between your eye and the lamp, and then hold the lens between the paper and the lamp. Move the lens closer to or farther away from the paper until the image of the lamp comes into focus on the waxed paper (Fig. 13).

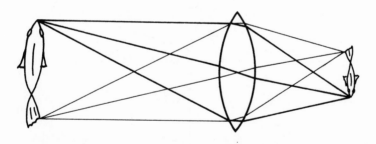

Fig. 12. *A lens focuses an image of the fish. The rays of light from each point on the fish are brought together at another point on the other side of the lens. The rays from the head are drawn in a heavy line and those from the tail are drawn in a light line to help you follow their paths through the lens.*

You probably will notice several differences between the images formed by a lens and those formed by a pinhole. One difference is that the image formed by the lens is much brighter than the image formed with a pinhole. This is because much more light comes through the lens than through the pinhole. For this reason the image of the lamp will be much more distinct, and you probably will be able to see more of the surroundings of the lamp. This is perhaps the major advantage of a lens over a pinhole: under ordinary conditions the image formed by a lens is much brighter and therefore more distinct than that formed by a pinhole.

There is a disadvantage to the lens that the pinhole does not have. With the lamp and the waxed paper in fixed positions, there is only one position in which you can hold the lens and still have the image of the lamp in sharp focus. If you move either the lamp or the waxed paper, the image goes out of focus and you have to adjust the position of the lens to bring it back into focus. With the lens at a given

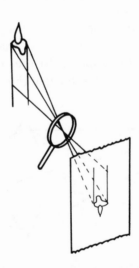

Fig. 13. *How to demonstrate focusing with a lens. You can use a lamp or a candle for this demonstration, but NEVER try to focus the image of the sun unless you want to start a fire. The concentration of bright light from the sun will cause paper to burn—sometimes within a few seconds.*

distance from the lamp, there is only one place on the other side of the lens, called the *plane of focus*, at which the image of the lamp will be in focus (Fig. 14). If you bring the waxed paper closer to the lens, the light rays from each point on the lamp will not yet have met; the image will not be in focus. Beyond the plane of focus the light rays diverge (spread apart), and if you place the waxed paper there, the image will not be in focus either. The farther from the plane of focus the waxed paper is, the less distinct will the image be.

With this information about lenses, we will consider one of the many eyes that focus with lenses—the human eye.

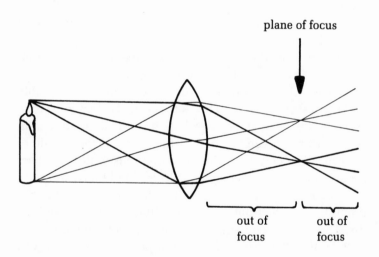

plane of focus

out of
focus

out of
focus

Fig. 14. *Only when the rays from a single point are brought together again, is the image of an object in focus. This place is called the plane of focus. Before and behind the plane of focus, the image is out of focus. If you hold your waxed paper near the plane of focus but not exactly at it, the image probably will be recognizable, but indistinct. The farther the paper is from the plane of focus, the more indistinct the image becomes.*

CHAPTER 4 / *The Human Eye*

THE PARTS OF THE HUMAN EYE that you can see by looking into someone else's eye or by looking into your own mirror are few (Fig. 15). To understand better how the eye works look at an imaginary section cut horizontally across an eye (Fig. 16).

The wall of the eye consists of three layers. The outer wall is a tough tissue that can withstand not only the pressure that exists within the normal eye, but considerably higher pressures as well. This outer layer is called the *sclera*, except in the front of the eye where it is called the *cornea*. In your mirror you can see part of the sclera as the "white of the eye." The cornea, which is continuous with the sclera, consists of living cells that are colorless and transparent.

The middle layer of the wall is the *choroid*, which continues toward the front of the eye as the *ciliary body* and the *iris*. The choroid contains blood vessels that bring nutrients to the retina. The *iris* is the colored part of the eye that you see in your mirror. Depending on the amount and location of the pigment within the iris, the iris may be blue, green, gray, or brown. The pigment absorbs light and protects the retina from excessive light. The black opening in the center of the iris is the *pupil*. The *ciliary body* supports the lens and also changes the shape of the lens when the eye changes its focus. The lens, like the cornea, consists of living, transparent cells, but it has a yellow color that absorbs ultraviolet light and prevents it from reaching the retina.

The inner layer of the wall of the eye is the *retina*. The human retina contains two types of photoreceptors called *rod cells* and *cone cells*. In addition the retina has neurons that transmit impulses to the brain by way of the *optic nerve* when the photoreceptors have been stimulated by light. Other neurons modify these impulses. Chapter 5 has more information about the retina.

Between the cornea and the iris is a chamber filled with a watery fluid called the *aqueous humor* (which means "watery fluid"). Behind the lens is a larger chamber filled with a thicker, jellylike material called the *vitreous*.

Light entering the eye passes through four transparent tissues or substances—the cornea, the aqueous humor, the lens, and the vitreous—before reaching the retina. Of these, the aqueous humor and the vitreous have almost no effect on the refracting of light rays. Most of the refraction—and, therefore, most of the focusing—of light is done by the cornea and the lens. The cornea is, in fact, a lens, though it usually is not called by that name. Nevertheless, it does most of the focusing in the eye. The cornea brings an image into focus near the retina, but not necessarily actually on the retina. If our eyes had corneas but no lenses, we probably would see somewhat fuzzy images of most objects. It is the lens that brings images into sharp focus on the retina of a normal eye. It is the lens that adjusts—or *accommodates*—

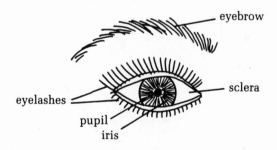

Fig. 15.   *The human eye as seen from the front.*

for the changing distances between the eye and the objects being viewed.

You will recall from using a magnifying glass to focus an image on waxed paper that the exact position of the lens is important. If you keep the waxed paper—which represents the retina in these experiments—in a fixed position but try to focus on near and distant objects, then you must move the magnifying glass closer to the waxed paper for distant objects and farther away for closer objects. When a distant object is in focus, a near object is out of focus. When a near object is in focus, a distant one is out of focus.

There are some resemblances between this and the way our eyes see. The lens of the eye focuses at only one distance at a time, although we usually don't notice this. This is because we ordinarily concentrate on whatever our eyes are most sharply focused on, and we ignore other things. Therefore we do not notice that those other things look indistinct to us. You can check this simply by trying to concentrate on what is out of focus for your eye. Select a tree or some other

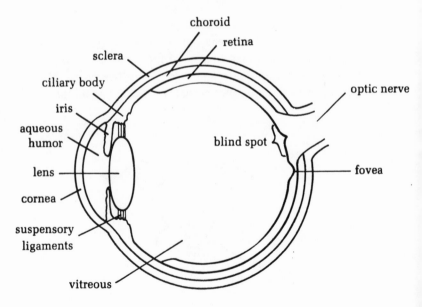

Fig. 16. *A section of the left eye. The section is cut horizontally across the eye, not from top to bottom.*

object in the distance. Then hold your finger along the line of sight between the tree and one eye and close the other eye. Bring the finger as close to your eye as you can and still see it in sharp focus; then with your eye still focusing on

Fig. 17. When your eye focuses on a near object, a distant object is out of focus (left). When you focus on a distant object, a near object is out of focus (right).

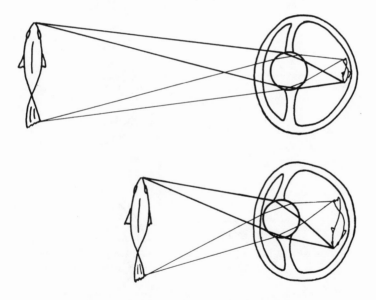

Fig. 18. When a fish eye focuses on distant objects, the lens moves backward in the eye (above). When a fish eye focuses on near objects, the lens moves forward in the eye (below).

your finger, try to concentrate on the tree. It should look rather indistinct (Fig. 17). Now focus your eye on the tree and try to concentrate on how your finger looks. The tree should be sharp and clear, but your finger will appear somewhat indistinct.

Now, how does an eye with a lens focus on objects? Some animal eyes—those of the octopus, squid, fishes, and amphibians—focus by moving the lens forward and backward (Fig. 18). In their eyes the lens moves forward when the eye focuses on near objects and backward when it focuses on distant objects.

There is, however, a second way that a lens can focus to different distances. The lenses in our own eyes and in the eyes of some other vertebrates (animals with backbones) focus by changing shape. The lens of the eye, unlike a glass lens, is composed of living cells, and it has a certain degree of elasticity, which the lens in the magnifying glass does not

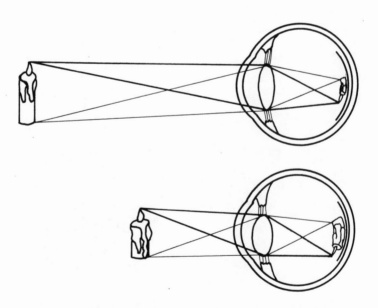

Fig. 19. *When the human eye focuses on distant objects the lens is flattened (above). When the human eye focuses on near objects the lens bulges (below).*

have. As the lens of the eye changes shape, so does the angle at which light rays strike the front surface and the rear surface of the lens, and this changes the angles of refraction as the light rays are bent. All this changes the location of the image formed by the lens (Fig. 19).

When the lens of a normal eye flattens, the image of a distant object is in focus on the retina; but the plane of focus of a near object lies behind the eyeball, and only an indistinct image of the near object reaches the retina. Because light rays do not pass through the wall of the eye, no sharp image of near objects is formed.

When the lens bulges, the image of a nearby object is in sharp focus on the retina. The image of a distinct object is in sharp focus somewhere in the vitreous body, and the light rays that continue on to the retina form only an indistinct one there.

The shape of the lens of the eye is determined by how much the *suspensory ligaments* pull on the lens. This, in turn, depends on the action of the muscles in the ciliary body (Fig. 20).

Muscle cells are long and slender. When they contract, they become shorter and thicker. When they relax, they become longer and thinner. In the ciliary body some muscle cells are attached at a point near the junction of the sclera and the cornea, and they extend backward toward the choroid. Another set of muscle cells in the ciliary body runs around the lens and suspensory ligaments. When all these muscle cells contract, they change the shape of the ciliary body in such a way that it extends closer to the lens; they also pull the ciliary body forward in the eye. All this shortens the distance between the ciliary body and the lens, thus reducing the tension of the suspensory ligaments and allowing the lens to bulge. The lens now brings near objects into focus.

When the muscles in the ciliary body relax, the ciliary body moves back to its former position, the suspensory ligaments exert more tension on the lens. Now the lens becomes flatter and brings distant objects into focus. From this, you can understand that when you read a book, the ciliary muscles are doing work, but when you look at a distant landscape, the muscles relax. That is why, after a prolonged period of reading or doing other close work, your eyes may feel tired.

As people grow older, the lens of the eye loses its elasticity, and so loses its ability to bulge. It remains in the flattened shape and makes the viewing of near objects diffi-

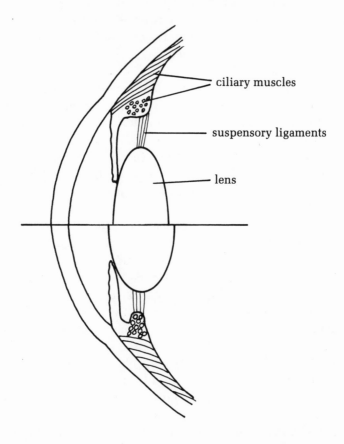

ciliary muscles

suspensory ligaments

lens

Fig. 20. When the muscles of the ciliary body relax, the suspensory ligaments pull on the lens, which then flattens (upper half of drawing). When the muscles of the ciliary body contract and become thicker, the suspensory ligaments no longer pull on the lens, which then bulges (lower half of drawing).

cult while distant objects may still be clearly visible. This condition is a type of *farsightedness* called *presbyopia*. It usually develops gradually. Some people in their thirties or forties begin at first to find that they must hold a book farther and farther away from their eyes to read it. Eventually, even at arm's length, a book is too close to be seen clearly. Corrective glasses can bring near objects into focus. In other persons presbyopia is so slight that they barely notice it, and their vision is nearly perfect even into old age.

Another type of *farsightedness* called *hypermetropia* (Fig. 21) is caused by having an eyeball that is shorter than normal. The plane of focus for near objects falls behind the retina when the ciliary muscles are relaxed. When the ciliary muscles in a normal eye contract, that image usually is brought far enough forward that the image falls on the retina, and the near object is seen clearly. But there is a limit to how much the ciliary muscles can contract, and with the short eye of farsighted persons, the muscles cannot contract enough to bring the image of near objects into focus on the retina.

Hypermetropia is corrected by wearing glasses with *convex lenses*—lenses that are thicker in the middle than at the edges. These lenses cause light rays to converge slightly before they enter the eye. This brings the image of a near object into focus on the retina.

In *nearsightedness*, or *myopia*, the eyeball is longer than normal (Fig. 21), and the sharp image of distant objects lies in the vitreous, but the image of near objects does come into focus on the retina. Persons who are nearsighted have difficulty with distance vision, but they usually can read books easily. Persons with extreme myopia may have to hold a book close to the eye for comfortable reading.

Myopia can be corrected by wearing glasses with *concave lenses*—lenses that are thicker near the edge than in the center. They cause light rays to diverge somewhat before they enter the eye. This brings the image of a distant object into focus on the retina.

In addition to the ciliary muscles that function in focusing, each eyeball has six muscles that function as three pairs

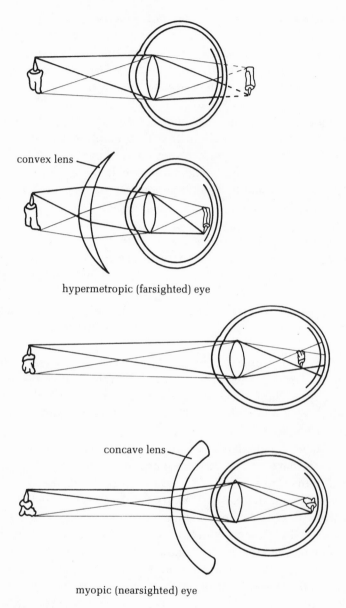

convex lens

hypermetropic (farsighted) eye

concave lens

myopic (nearsighted) eye

Fig. 21. Convex glasses correct hypermetropia, a type of farsightedness (upper half). Concave glasses correct myopia, or nearsightedness (lower half). See text for more details.

in moving the eye: one pair moves the eye up and down, one pair moves it from side to side, and the other pair rotates it. These muscles are illustrated in Figure 22.

When the *superior rectus* (a rectus is a straight muscle) contracts, it moves the eye upward; when the *inferior rectus* contracts, it moves the eye down. Usually the superior rectus muscles of the two eyes contract at the same time, and both inferior rectus muscles contract at the same time. Because of the way these muscles are coordinated, we cannot move one eye up or down at a time; both eyes move up or down together.

The *medial rectus* moves the eye toward the nose, and the *lateral rectus* moves the eye away from the nose. If you wish to look to one side, then the medial rectus of one eye and the lateral rectus of the other eye contract simultaneously. Although you cannot make your eyes diverge—that is, you cannot make your left eye look to the left while your right eye looks to the right—they ordinarily can converge to some extent when you are focusing on a single small object. How much they converge depends on how near the object is that you are viewing. If it is several hundred feet away, the convergence is negligible. But as you read this book, both

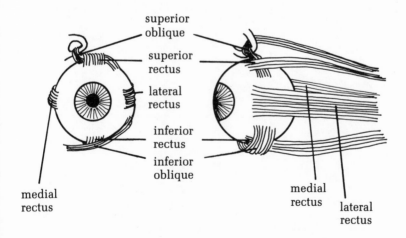

Fig. 22.   Muscles that move the eyeball. These are two views of a left eye.

medial rectus muscles contract somewhat and cause your eyes to converge on the printed words. If you bring a finger close to your nose and manage to keep your eyes converged on the finger, you will have a cross-eyed appearance. This unusual degree of muscle contraction is uncomfortable enough that you don't voluntarily keep your eyes crossed very long.

If you stand with your head upright, the scene before you looks upright. If you tilt your head a little to one side, the scene still appears upright. This is because two more muscles, the *superior oblique* and the *inferior oblique* can rotate the eye somewhat. This keeps the images in the two eyes on corresponding parts of the retinas, and your brain can interpret them as one image.

There is a limit to how much eyes can be rotated. If you lie on your side with your head horizontal, everything will look as if it is perpendicular to the way it was before— though, of course, it is actually you who are perpendicular to your former position.

CHAPTER 5 / *The Retina*

THE RETINA OF THE HUMAN EYE contains not only the photoreceptor cells, but a number of other cells as well. They are arranged in four layers. Beginning with those nearest the choroid and ending with those nearest the vitreous, they are

1. pigment epithelium cells
2. photoreceptors (rod cells and cone cells)
3. bipolar cells, horizontal cells, and amacrine cells
4. ganglion cells (parts of which form the optic nerve)

Figure 23 is diagrammatic and is a somewhat simplified cross section of a human retina. In a real retina the cells are packed much more closely together—so much so that it would be difficult to follow each cell in a drawing that showed them all. Notice that light must pass through most of the retina before reaching the photoreceptors. Because most of the retina cells are transparent, very little light is lost this way.

The *pigment epithelium cells* contain granules of a black pigment called *melanin*. Melanin absorbs whatever light has passed through the photoreceptors and has not been absorbed by them. This means that almost no light is reflected back into the eye again. If this were to happen, the light might strike photoreceptors in another part of the eye and this would blur the image (Fig. 24).

Because the pigment epithelium absorbs nearly all the

light reaching it, it is black. This is why the pupil of the eye appears black, for when you look into someone's eyes, you are looking through the pupil toward the pigment epithelium.

The pigment cells have long, fingerlike projections or processes, as they are called, that extend between the photoreceptors. In dim light the melanin granules remain in the

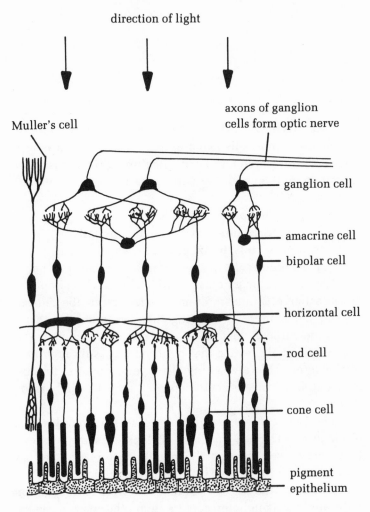

Fig. 23. *Cross section of the retina taken from an area that has both rods and cones.*

main part of the cell. In bright light the processes grow in length and the pigment granules move into the processes; this probably prevents the reflection or refraction of light rays from one photoreceptor to another.

Because the photoreceptor cells die when the nearby pigment epithelium cells die, the pigment epithelium probably plays a vital role in the life of the photoreceptor cells.

Most of the cells of the retina (the photoreceptor, bipolar, horizontal, amacrine, and ganglion cells) are nerve cells —or *neurons*—that conduct nervous impulses. Most neurons have three parts: *dendrite, cell body,* and *axon* (Fig. 25). Of these, the dendrite and the axon usually are long and

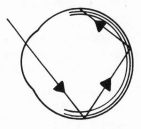

Fig. 24. *How light might be reflected within the eye if there were no dark pigment epithelium that absorbed light after its first passage through the retina.*

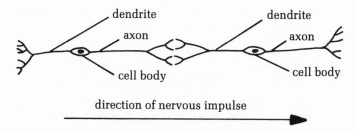

direction of nervous impulse

Fig. 25. *Two neurons. In nearly all nervous tissue in the body, nervous impulses travel from dendrite to cell body to axon in one neuron, then to the dendrite of the next neuron.*

slender and look threadlike even under an ordinary microscope, although their tips are often branched rather pro-
fusely. The cell body, which contains the nucleus of the
neuron, is wider than the rest of the cell. Neurons often have
several—even many—dendrites, but only one cell body and
only one axon. The movement of nervous impulses ordinarily is from dendrite to cell body to axon. Where the axon of
one neuron meets the dendrite of another, the impulse
passes to the second neuron. Because the axons of many
neurons may meet the dendrites of one neuron, and because
a branching axon may meet the dendrites of several neurons,
in some instances nervous impulses take quite complicated
pathways. Some of the pathways followed by nervous impulses in the retina are well known; others we understand
only imperfectly.

Nervous impulses in the retina are initiated in the photoreceptor cells. The two types of photoreceptor cells in the
human eye are the *rod cells* and *cone cells*. The dendrites of
rod cells are rod-shaped and are called *rods*. The dendrites
of cone cells are roughly cone-shaped—though it may take
a little imagination to see this in some cone cells—and these
dendrites are called *cones*. It is the rods and cones that are
the photoreceptors; even more specifically it is certain pigments, the visual pigments, which are confined to certain
membranes in the rods and cones, that are photoreceptive.

Like other living cells, the rod and cone cells are surrounded by a membrane called the *plasma membrane* (or
cell membrane). In the rods, the plasma membrane folds
inward and bits of the membrane are pinched off, forming
flat disks called *thylakoids* (Fig. 26). As new thylakoids are
formed near the base of a rod, the older ones are pushed
toward the opposite end. There they slough off and are en-
gulfed by the pigment epithelium cells, which digest them.

In the human eye there are several hundred thylakoids
in each rod; they are stacked like a pile of coins—one on top
of the other. Since the visual pigment is in the thylakoid
membranes, light rays pass through hundreds of layers of
visual pigments. This arrangement of thylakoids makes it
much more likely that light will actually strike visual pig-

ments than it would if there were only one or two thylakoids in a rod. Because the striking of a visual pigment by light is what initiates vision, this stacking of thylakoids makes vision more sure.

The visual pigment in rods is *rhodopsin.* It is also called *visual purple,* which is not really the best name for it, because it is red. Rhodopsin is sensitive to visible light of all colors, though it is most sensitive to green and least sensitive to red. When a rod in your eye is struck by visible light of any wavelength, you have the sensation of seeing white light. If you had only rods in your retinas—as some animals do—you would be totally colorblind and see the world much as you see a black and white movie.

Rhodopsin is also sensitive to ultraviolet light, but because the lens absorbs ultraviolet light, ultraviolet rarely reaches the retina.

In cones, the thylakoids do not pinch off from the plasma membrane but remain as inward turning parts of the membrane (Fig. 26). Nonetheless, as in rods, the layers of membrane are stacked one on top of the other.

There are three types of cones in the human retina. Each contains a visual pigment similar to rhodopsin, but not exactly the same. One of these pigments absorbs mostly blue light and very little light of other colors. Another pigment

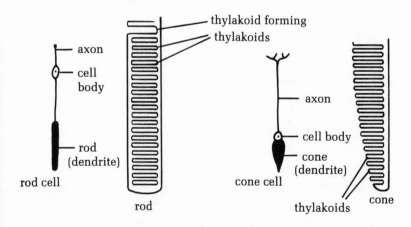

Fig. 26. *Details of rods and cones. Diagrammatic.*

absorbs mostly green, and the third absorbs mostly red light. If only one type of cone is stimulated, we see only the corresponding color. If, for instance, only blue light reaches the retina, cones with the blue-sensitive pigment are strongly stimulated, the other cones slightly or not at all. Then we have the sensation of seeing blue. Similarly, when only green light or only red light shines on the retina, the corresponding cones are stimulated, and we have the sensation of seeing green or red. If all three types of cone are stimulated in approximately equal proportions, we see white.

Of course, we see many more colors than these. This happens when two types of cone are stimulated (in either equal or unequal proportions) or when all three types are stimulated in varying proportions.

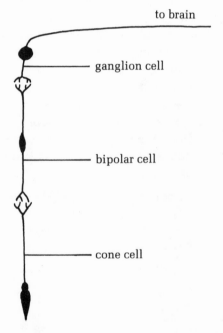

Fig. 27.   The most direct route a nervous impulse can take from the retina to the brain is: photoreceptor (cone cell or rod cell) to bipolar cell to ganglion cell. The axon of the ganglion cell extends the length of the optic nerve and enters the brain.

When light strikes pigment in a rod or a cone, a nervous impulse is set up that travels through the cell body and axon of that neuron. From here the impulse might travel along a bipolar cell, and then along a ganglion cell. The axons of the ganglion cells form the optic nerve, which leads to the brain. This pathway from rod or cone cell to bipolar cell to ganglion cell is the most nearly direct path from photoreceptor to brain that a nervous impulse in the eye can take (Fig. 27). We will consider some other paths later in this chapter.

Rods and cones are not distributed uniformly throughout the retina. At the center of the retina is a small depression called the *fovea centralis,* or merely the *fovea* (Fig. 16). Here there are cones but no rods. Around the fovea there are both cones and rods, but the greater the distance from the fovea, the fewer the cones. Near the edge of the retina there are no cones—only rods.

Because of this, *how* we see something depends on where within the retina the image falls. If the image falls on the fovea, we see the object in color; if the image falls near

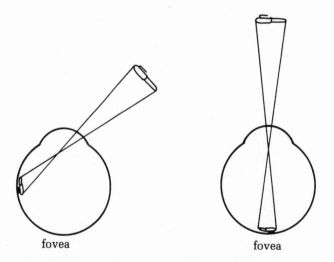

fovea   fovea

Fig. 28.   *The image of an object just barely within the field of vision falls on an area of the retina that has only rods (left). If the object is in the center of the field of vision, the image falls on the fovea, which has only cones (right).*

the edge of the retina, we see it only in shades of black, gray, and white. If the image falls in an intermediate area, we see color more or less distinctly depending on the proportion of rods and cones in that area.

You can see this easily yourself by performing a simple experiment. Get a set of objects of similar size and shape but of different colors—perhaps a set of felt or ballpoint pens that are color coded or just some pieces of colored paper. Hold them behind your back where you can't see them and select one at random with your right hand. With your left eye closed and with your right eye looking straight ahead, bring the object to eye level but so far back that you still can't see it. Then slowly bring it forward until it is barely visible. Be sure to look forward all the time. The object probably will look black or gray to you at first because the image will fall first on the rod-rich edge of the retina.

Continue to move the object forward. When the image reaches an area with cones you will begin to see color, but you might be mistaken about *which* color it is. As the image comes into areas with more and more cones, you will be able to make an accurate determination of color (Fig. 28).

There is another difference between the fovea and the rest of the retina, and this is in the number of photoreceptors that converge on bipolar cells and the number of bipolar cells that converge on ganglion cells. In the fovea, there is one bipolar cell per cone cell and one ganglion cell per bipolar cell. Therefore, if light shines on, let us say, a hundred cones, then a hundred separate nervous impulses are sent simultaneously to the brain. In other parts of the retina, several rods converge on one bipolar cell, and several bipolar cells converge on one ganglion cell. In some areas of the retina as many as 600 rods send their impulses to the brain —by way of bipolar cells—through one ganglion cell. Therefore, if light shines on all 600 rods, only one nervous impulse is sent to the brain. For this reason, vision is most acute in the fovea and less acute elsewhere (Fig. 29). We might draw an analogy with the process of preparing a picture composed only of dots. If you use a pen with a fine point that makes very small dots, you can get many more dots to the square inch, and your picture can show a great deal of fine detail. If you use a pen with a wide point that makes large dots, a picture of the same size cannot have so much detail and so will be less distinct.

The fovea, therefore, sends a finely detailed "picture" to the brain, and the edge of the retina sends a poorly detailed one. You can check this by bringing a ruler or some other object with fine markings slowly into the field of vision of one eye—as you did with the colored objects. You probably

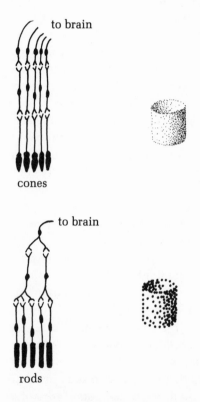

Fig. 29. *If each photoreceptor transmits a separate impulse to the brain, vision is most acute (above). If several photoreceptors share one ganglion cell, then only one impulse at a time can be sent to the brain even though all the photoreceptors may be stimulated by light at the same time; then vision is less acute (below).*

will have to bring it close to the center of your field of vision before you can read the markings well. Again, don't succumb to the temptation to look directly at the ruler; keep staring straight ahead. For a variation on this experiment, look directly at one letter in the middle of a paragraph in this book. How many words can you read without moving your eye? Probably not many.

What we see in color and in best detail, then, are those objects whose images fall on the fovea of the retina. Because we nearly always move our eyes or heads (or both) to bring objects of interest into the center of our field of vision, their images automatically fall on the fovea. Because our minds concentrate on these objects of interest, we ordinarily don't notice that we see other things less distinctly.

Although rod vision is less acute than cone vision, it does have one advantage over cone vision: rods are more sensitive to light. They can be stimulated by light that is much too faint to stimulate cones. Probably this is because the visual pigments in the cones are much more dilute than is the rhodopsin in the rods. With only cones in our retinas we would be virtually blind in very dim light, whereas with rods as well as cones, we do see at least something at night. Of course, we don't see as well as we do by day, and there are at least three reasons for this.

One reason is that, because rods do not distinguish color, in very dim light we do not see color. If you find some place without any artificial illumination and stand there as the sun goes down and night comes on, the colors of objects around you will gradually fade. You might want to watch the colors in a set of crayons or colored pens.

A second reason we don't see as well in dim light as in bright light is that there are no rods in the fovea. Therefore, in very dim light, when the cones are not working, we actually cannot see what is in the center of our field of vision. Because we are so accustomed to looking directly at an object of interest by day, we automatically look directly at such an object at night. But if the light is so dim that the cones are not functioning, it is best to look slightly to the side of an object. This way the image falls on the rods and not the cones. Some clear night, when stars are visible, locate moderately faint star. Look directly at it, then slightly to one side of it. It should appear to be brighter when you look away. Now look for fainter and fainter stars. You ought to be able to find a few that are so faint they disappear when you look directly at them and reappear when you look slightly to the side.

The features associated with rod vision—lack of color, not seeing what we look directly at, and less acuteness of vision—are certainly inconvenient. But some vision in dim light is certainly much better than none at all, and it is our rods that let us see under these conditions.

Fig. 30. *Follow the directions in the text to demonstrate your blind spot.*

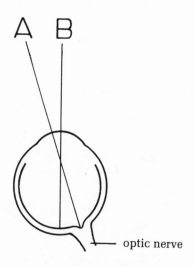

optic nerve

Fig. 31. *If the letters are at the proper distance to demonstrate the blind spot, the image of A will fall on the blind spot when the image of B falls on the fovea.*

In the retina of each eye, there is one spot where the axons of all the ganglion cells meet and form the optic nerve. This spot contains no photoreceptors. Because we cannot see any light that falls here, this spot is called the blind spot (Fig. 16). In the left eye it is somewhat to the right of the fovea, and in the right eye it is to the left of the fovea. Therefore, in the field of vision of each eye there is actually a spot in which we can see nothing. However, we are almost never aware of our blind spots. Yet they are easy to demonstrate, provided you do it one eye at a time. Just close your right eye and hold Figure 30 a foot or more from your face. With your left eye look directly at the letter B. The letter A will be visible. Now slowly bring the book closer to your face while always looking directly at B with your left eye. When the book reaches approximately eight inches from your face, the A will disappear because its image then will fall on the blind spot (Fig. 31). Be sure not to give in to the temptation to look directly at A, for then it will not disappear.

To demonstrate the blind spot in your right eye, close your left eye and look directly at the A with your right eye. When the page is about eight inches from your face the B will disappear.

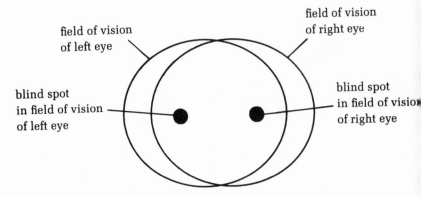

Fig. 32.   One reason our blind spots are not noticeable ordinarily is that the field of vision of each eye overlaps that part of the field of vision of the other eye that contains the blind spot.

One reason that we ordinarily don't notice our blind spots is that the blind spots of both eyes do not coincide. Where the blind spot lies in the field of vision of one eye, the other eye has clear vision (Fig. 32).

But this is not the entire explanation, for if you close one eye and look at a room or read a book with the other eye, you probably won't notice the blind spot in the open eye either. This is because the blind spot is off center in the eye, and we don't pay much attention to images that are not on or near the fovea.

So far we have skipped over two types of neurons in the retina: the *horizontal cells* and the *amacrine cells*. These cells lie approximately at right angles to the neurons we have already discussed.

Horizontal cells extend from photoreceptor (rod or cone cell) to photoreceptor, usually at the point at which the re-

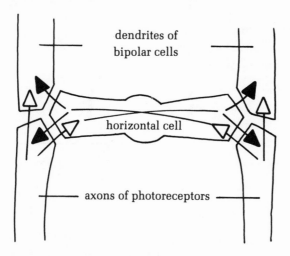

dendrites of
bipolar cells

horizontal cell

axons of photoreceptors

Fig. 33. *Horizontal cells are unusual in that they can receive and transmit impulses at both ends. Therefore neither end of the cell can be properly called dendrite or axon. When a horizontal cell receives an impulse from a photoreceptor, it may transmit an inhibitory impulse to another photoreceptor and/or its bipolar cell. White arrowheads: stimulatory impulses. Black arrowheads: inhibitory impulses.*

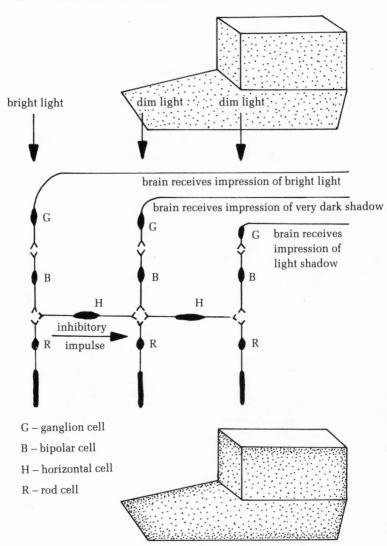

Fig. 34. *Contrast detection. Although the shadow of a box may be uniformly gray (above), the edges of the shadow appear darker to us (below) because a horizontal cell carries inhibitory impulses from the brightly illuminated retinal cells to the retinal cells on which the edge of the image of the shadow falls. More distant cells in the shaded area are not inhibited.*

ceptor axon meets the dendrite of a bipolar cells; this makes a three-way junction. It is believed that at one of these junctions impulses can flow in the following directions:

photoreceptor to bipolar cell
photoreceptor to horizontal cell
horizontal cell to photoreceptor
horizontal cell to bipolar cell

Ordinarily impulses flow in only one direction between neurons—from the axon of one neuron to the dendrite of the next. It is unusual for nervous impulses to flow in two directions, but this is what happens between photoreceptors and horizontal cells (Fig. 33).

Horizontal cells probably function by increasing our perception of contrast between light and dark areas. If you look at a shadow cast, let us say, by a box lying on a piece of white paper, the shadow appears to be a little darker near its edge even though it really is uniformly gray. This slightly darker edge makes the shadow just a little more noticeable to you. It is believed that a horizontal cell that receives an impulse from a photoreceptor can send an inhibitory impulse to another photoreceptor or to the bipolar cell associ-

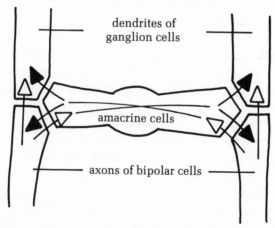

Fig. 35. *Like the horizontal cells of Figure 33, amacrine cells transmit inhibitory impulses in both directions. In this case, they inhibit the passage of nervous impulses before or just after they reach ganglion cells.*

ated with it. This blocks any impulses that might otherwise have been sent by the second photoreceptor cell to the brain (Fig. 34). The photoreceptors in the edge of the image of shadow will be inhibited more frequently than those farther away. Hence, the shadow appears darker at its edge.

This enhancing of contrast makes objects more noticeable to us, for objects not only cast shadows, but one side of an object is usually shaded—and some objects have both brightly and darkly colored areas. The ability to detect contrast makes it easier for us to see things that are not moving —for instance, a coin or ring dropped on a pebbled walk. This ability must have helped our ancestors when they looked for the kind of food that does not move much—fruits hidden among the leaves of a tree, for instance. It probably also helped them to detect predators lying in wait.

Amacrine cells, like horizontal cells, extend horizontally in the retina. They make three-way junctions with bipolar cells and ganglion cells (Fig. 35). It is believed that at one of these junctions impulses can flow in the following directions:

> bipolar cell to ganglion cell
> bipolar cell to amacrine cell
> amacrine cell to bipolar cell
> amacrine cell to ganglion cell

Here, as in the three-way junctions involving horizontal cells, some impulses are inhibitory. In studies of the retina of the mudpuppy (a type of salamander), it was found that amacrine cells would inhibit ganglion cells—but only when a light was turned on or off—not while the light was on. The amacrine cells thus seem to be involved in detecting a change in the intensity of light reaching the photoreceptors. Such a change in light intensity can happen when an object being viewed moves, especially if that object is lighter or darker than its background. As an image crosses the retina, amacrine cells are stimulated only when the leading and trailing edges of the image go by. A moving shadow would create the same effect.

Amacrine cells, therefore, are believed to be movement detectors. They are of value in detecting moving prey or a moving predator. Some of our ancestors must have owed their lives to seeing just one small movement of a leopard or other predator about to pounce from its hiding place. Some of us may still be alive today because we caught one quick glimpse of an automobile speeding around a corner. We also use movement detection in action sports like football or tennis. Sometimes we judge our own motion by the apparent motion of things that really stand still; a skier, for instance, can judge his relative speed by how rapidly trees seem to be rushing backward as their images move across his retina.

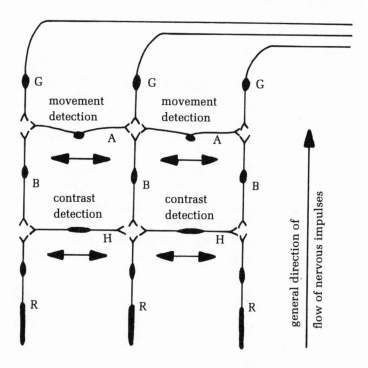

Fig. 36. *Summary of the flow of nervous impulses in the retina. The general direction of movement of impulses is from photoreceptors to bipolar cells to ganglion cells (large arrow) and then to the brain. This movement can be inhibited by impulses carried by horizontal or amacrine cells. These inhibitory impulses move horizontally (two-headed arrows).*

In addition to the cells described thus far in this chapter, Muller's cells occupy spaces among the other cells of the retina. Muller's cells are filled with glycogen (a starch-like substance) and probably nourish the neurons of the retina.

If the discussion in this chapter makes the retina seem complicated, you should know that it is even more complicated. The diagrams in this chapter are very much simplified, for each neuron in a real retina is connected to many more neurons than are shown here. Much more is known about the functioning of the retina than could possibly be put into one small chapter. In addition, much more remains to be learned about the retina than we know now. Nevertheless, we can summarize the general flow of information through the retina in a few statements:

1. The general direction of nervous impulse is through three types of neuron in the following order: photoreceptor (rod or cone cell) to bipolar cell to ganglion cell.

2. Horizontal cells are involved in contrast detection; they function by inhibiting impulses as they flow from photoreceptor to bipolar cell.

3. Amacrine cells are involved in movement detection; they function by inhibiting impulses as they flow from bipolar cell to ganglion cell.

You might want to compare these three statements with Figure 36, which summarizes the same information in diagrammatic form.

CHAPTER 6 / *Adapting to Light and Dark*

HUMAN EYES SERVE human activities, now and as they once were. Eyes of other animals are like or unlike human eyes, depending on the normal lives and needs of those animals. Most animals that survive, survive because their bodies are well adapted to their instinctive patterns of life or vice-versa.

The intensity of light any animal receives varies from time to time and from place to place, and animals that are active at only certain times and in certain places have eyes adapted to the intensities that they are most likely to encounter in their natural habitats. For convenience we might divide animals into four groups on the basis of these adaptations: nocturnal, diurnal, crepuscular, and arrhythmic. However, you must remember that there are no sharp demarcations among these groups.

NOCTURNAL ANIMALS

Strictly *nocturnal animals* (rats, mice, and lemurs, for example) normally are active only at night and sleep in dark places by day. Some nocturnal animals have eyes that see poorly or not at all; these animals possess some combination of other senses—smell, hearing, or touch—so well developed that they can find food and escape from danger without the use of vision. Perhaps the most extreme examples of this are the blind animals that live their entire lives in caves where light never penetrates. Without light, eyes are useless.

Blind nocturnal animals need not concern us here, since they do not see; but some of the strictly nocturnal animals that can see rather well by the dim light of night are interesting. Their eyes have various combinations of adaptations that make efficient use of the little light that reaches them. The photoreceptors in their retinas are all or nearly all rods. Cones would be useless at night, when the animal is about, and equally useless by day, when the animal sleeps. Rods, which are much more sensitive to light, make more efficient use of what light there is than cones would. The retina has no cone-rich fovea as our eyes do; rather, this area, which corresponds to the center of the field of vision, contains rods. The animal, then, can look directly at a very dimly lit object and see it much better than we would if we looked directly at it on a dark night.

rat

flying squirrel

Fig. 37. *Nocturnal animals typically have large, bulging eyes.*

The eyes of nocturnal animals usually have one or more features that increase the amount of light that comes in. These include pupils that open wide, eyes that are large in proportion to the size of the head, and corneas that bulge outward (Fig. 37).

A pupil that opens wide allows more light to reach the retina and so makes a brighter image. Because doubling the diameter of a circle increases its area four times, and because the amount of light passing through the pupil is propor-

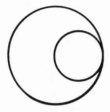

Fig. 38. *If the diameter of a circle is doubled, its area is* quadrupled.

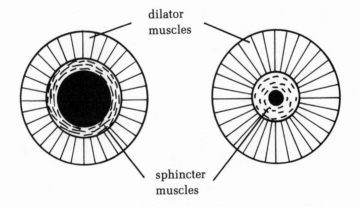

dilator
muscles

sphincter
muscles

Fig. 39. *When dilator muscle cells contract (shorten) and* *sphincter muscle cells relax, the pupil is large. When* *dilator muscle cells relax, and sphincter muscle cells* *contract, the pupil becomes smaller. These changes occur* *automatically as the intensity of light reaching the eye* *changes.*

tional to its area, doubling the diameter of the pupil increases by four times the brightness of the image on the retina (Fig. 38). Because a large eye can have a large iris, and therefore also a large pupil, it is usually advantageous for a nocturnal animal to have as large an eye as possible without, of course, its being so large that other parts of the head are left without enough room.

When a nocturnal animal moves into brighter light, the pupil closes down. Most strictly nocturnal animals have round pupils that are opened and closed by two kinds of muscles in the iris: *dilator muscles* and *sphincter muscles* (Fig. 39). The cells of the dilator muscle lie across the iris, and the cells of the sphincter muscle encircle the pupil. When the dilator muscle cells contract (shorten), the sphincter muscle cells relax; this dilates, or enlarges, the pupil. When the sphincter muscle cells contract, they become shorter and thicker, and this makes the pupil smaller; at the same time the dilator muscle cells relax.

Because there is a limit to how much a muscle can shorten when it contracts, a round pupil cannot close completely, for the cells next to the pupil would then have to shrink down to a length of almost nothing. The inability of the round pupil to close completely is of no inconvenience to the animal in the dark, but strictly nocturnal animals are uncomfortable in sunlight and usually will seek darkness when placed in bright light. There are some nocturnal animals that are not strictly nocturnal; that is, they are active to some extent by day or they prefer to sleep in the warmth of direct sunlight. Most of these animals have slit pupils that close completely or nearly so. These are discussed later in this chapter.

You might think that the closing down of a pupil would reduce the field of vision, but this is not necessarily so. Compare Figures 12 and 40. If a barrier with a hole in it is placed between the fish and the lens in such a position that at least some rays from all parts of the fish reach the lens, then a complete image of the fish will be formed. However, the image will be fainter because the barrier prevents some of the light rays from reaching the plane of focus.

To demonstrate this, get your magnifying glass, waxed paper, and cardboard. Cut two round holes of different sizes —perhaps ¼ inch and 1 inch in diameter. The holes should be a few inches apart. On a sunny day hold the magnifying glass and the waxed paper so as to focus the image of the view outside your window. Examine the image for a few moments so that you become familiar with all the objects in it. Now hold the cardboard with the larger hole on the far side of the magnifying glass from you. The cardboard should touch the glass, and the hole should be centered on the glass (Fig. 41). You probably can hold the cardboard and magnifying glass this way with one hand and hold the waxed paper in the other. Now bring the image of the scene into focus on the waxed paper. The image will be dimmer than before, but it should be just as large. Now replace the large hole with the smaller hole. The image will be even darker but should still include everything that you saw in the first image.

In this demonstration the magnifying glass represents the lens of the eye, the cardboard represents the iris, and the holes represent the pupil opened to different widths. There is at least one point at which the comparison does not hold, however. You can change the size of the hole in the cardboard at will—even though the intensity of light in the scene

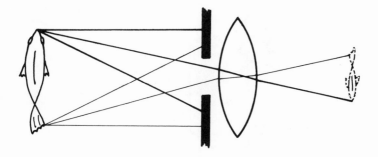

Fig. 40.   *If some of the light rays from an object are blocked before they reach a lens, an image of the entire object may be formed, but the image will be dim unless the object is very bright.*

does not change. Or, you can choose to use the same hole when the light intensity does change. The real pupil in our own eyes and in the eyes of many other animals does not act like this. A pupil usually opens automatically as the light dims, and it closes automatically as the light becomes brighter. This tends to keep the brightness of the image on the retina more or less constant.

Some nocturnal animals also have an area in their eyes called the *tapetum lucidum*, which means "bright carpet." The eyes of many animals have the same black pigment epithelium as we have, which absorbs light that has passed

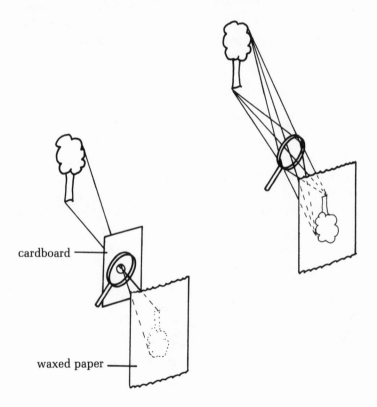

Fig. 41. *How to demonstrate that blocking some light rays need not prevent the formation of an image, but that it will make the image less bright. Keep the cardboard against the magnifying glass.*

through the retina unabsorbed and so prevents its being reflected back and forth within the eye and blurring the image on the retina. However, a small area near the back of the eye of some nocturnal animals contains cells that reflect light forward through the retina (Fig. 42). This tissue, the tapetum lucidum, is actually a small mirror. As the light passes a second time through a photoreceptor, there is another chance that it will be absorbed by the visual pigment. This increases the animal's ability to see in dim light.

Any light reflected from the tapetum lucidum that passes unabsorbed through the retina continues out of the eye. This light, sometimes called *eyeshine*, can be seen as a light shining out of the eyes of some nocturnal animals. You can see it best if the animal is in darkness while a single light behind and a little to one side of your head shines in the animal's eyes. Then the eyes look as if they had their own source of light glowing inside them, but, of course, it is merely reflected light that you see. People with pet cats often see eyeshine when a cat sits in a darkened room and faces a brightly lit one. Along a dark road at night some animal in the distance may be visible only as two eyes reflecting the light of automobile headlights.

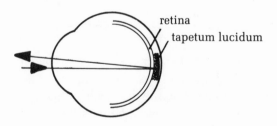

Fig. 42. *The tapetum lucidum (shown crosshatched here) is a tissue that reflects light much as a mirror does. The reflected light passes through the retina a second time.*

DIURNAL ANIMALS

Diurnal animals (chickens, canaries, and squirrels, for instance) sleep at night and are active by day, when the light is often bright enough to damage unprotected photoreceptors. The eyes of these animals have adaptations that reduce the intensity of light reaching the photoreceptors. We, ourselves, are usually classified as diurnal with reference to the adaptations of our eyes although we can see a little better at night than some strictly diurnal animals can.

In general, the eyes of diurnal animals have characteristics that are the opposite of those of nocturnal animals. Most have cones, which are less sensitive to light than are

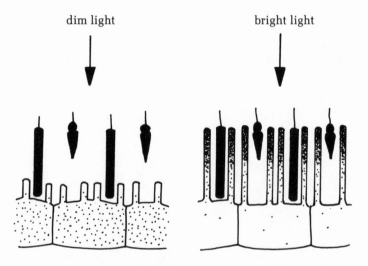

dim light   bright light

Fig. 43. *Adaptation to changes in light intensities by the human eye. In dim light (left), the processes of the pigment epithelium are short and the dark pigment granules are nearly all confined to the main body of the cell. In bright light (right), the processes elongate and the pigment granules move into them. Because in a real retina the cells are much more crowded than shown here, the protection provided by the movement of pigment granules is greater than this diagram suggests.*

rods, and so do not need as much protection from light as rods do. Cones can also provide color vision, though it is not clear how many animals with cones actually can distinguish one color from another. Some diurnal animals, such as ground squirrels, goldfish, many birds, and some lizards and snakes, have only cones and no rods at all. Such animals are virtually blind in very dim light and usually rest throughout the dark hours. Some, like ourselves, have both rods and cones and can see enough to get along if the night is not too dark, though they would prefer to be active only by day.

Diurnal animals usually have smaller, flatter lenses than do nocturnal animals, and their corneas do not bulge so much. Each of these features reduces the brightness of the image on the retina, but the lens and the cornea do form a relatively large image there. Because a large image falls over many rods and cones, the detail can be very fine.

CREPUSCULAR ANIMALS

Crepuscular animals are active only at dusk—for a short time after sunset or before sunrise or both. These animals can see well only within a narrow range of light intensity that appears somewhat dim to us. Their eyes have no special adaptations that either would increase their efficiency in very low light intensities or would protect their eyes from very bright light.

ARRHYTHMIC ANIMALS

Finally, there are animals that can be active by both day and night. Horses, cattle, and other hoofed animals, which may be preyed upon at any time of day or night, are awake and alert nearly all the time and sleep for only short periods scattered throughout the 24-hour day. Such animals have been called *arrhythmic* (which means "not rhythmic"). It is perhaps unfortunate that this term was applied to these animals, for all animals exhibit daily rhythms of several sorts.

It must be understood that this term is meant to refer here only to the ability of the eyes to see well by both night and day.

The eyes of arrhythmic animals usually possess some combination of nocturnal and diurnal adaptations. They may have, for instance, both rods and cones, the rods functioning primarily in dim light, the cones primarily in bright light. The proportion of rods to cones varies from species to species.

The retina itself affords some protection from bright light to the photoreceptors, especially to the rods. The cells of the pigment epithelium of human beings and many other animals bear fingerlike extensions or processes that occur between the rods and cones (Figures 23 and 43). In dim light, these processes are relatively short, but in bright light

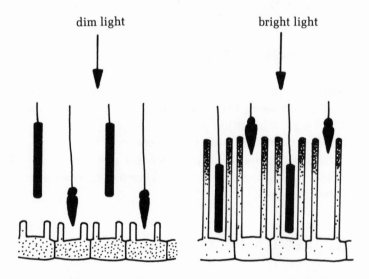

Fig. 44. *The retina of an amphibian adapts to changing light intensity as does the human retina (Fig. 43), but in addition, the rods and cones themselves move. In dim light (left), the rods, which are most sensitive to light are nearest the light. In bright light (right), the cones, which are least likely to be damaged by it, move forward, and the rods move back into the protection of the pigment epithelium.*

they elongate and extend a greater distance between the rods and cones. At the same time, the pigment granules in the cells move into the processes. The pigment granules absorb light, and this offers the rods some protection from the bright light. When dim light returns, the processes shorten, and the pigment granules move back into the main body of the pigment epithelium cells.

In the eyes of frogs, toads, and some fishes, there is, in addition to this action of the pigment epithelium, a movement of rods and cones within the retina when light conditions change (Fig. 44). In dim light, the cones are near the pigment epithelium, and the rods are near the light. In bright light, the rods move back toward the pigment epithelium— where they are partially shaded by the pigment granules— and the cones, which function best in bright light, move toward the light.

Both of these movements—the movement of pigment cell granules and the movement of rods and cones—are relatively slow; they take at least a few minutes and sometimes longer. A more rapid adaptation to changing light intensity is the opening and closing of the pupil. In arrhythmic animals, as in other animals, the closing of the pupil to a small opening in bright light decreases greatly the amount of light entering the eye and protects the rods from bright light. The decrease in pupil size also increases the sharpness of the image, which, combined with the presence of cones, makes

Fig. 45. *Spherical aberration. The light rays passing through the lens of the eye do not all come to a perfect focus at one point (above). If the iris closes down a bit (below), some of the light rays are eliminated, and the remaining points of focus are spread over a smaller area, and this improves the acuity of our vision. The distance between the points of focus is exaggerated in this drawing.*

the daytime vision of many diurnal and arrhythmic animals very acute.

A small pupil opening increases acuity because the lens of the eye does not focus light perfectly. The illustrations you have seen thus far in this book have shown light rays coming from a single point meeting again at another single point after passing through a lens, but this is not altogether true. The light rays that pass through the lens near its edge come together a little closer to the lens than do those light rays that pass through near the center of the lens. This phenomenon is called *spherical aberration*. It is exaggerated somewhat in Figure 45.

When the pupil closes down, the light rays that would have reached the outer part of the lens are blocked off. This decreases the amount of spherical aberration, for the light rays that do pass through the lens are nearly in focus at the same point.

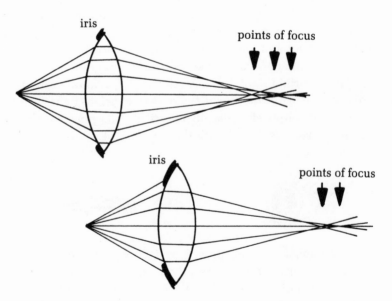

Fig. 46. *By bringing our eyelids closer together, we can reduce the effective size of the pupil opening and therefore increase acuity of vision. This is most effective in bright light.*

You might like to perform the following demonstration. Get a piece of cardboard with one pinhole about 1 millimeter across. With one eye open, find something that is too near or too far away to be perfectly clear to you. You might hold a page of this book so close to your eye that the letters just begin to look fuzzy. Now bring the pinhole close to your eye. What you see should be much clearer. Repeat, using holes of various sizes in the cardboard. The smaller the hole, the sharper the image (unless you make extremely small holes, in which case another phenomenon, called *diffraction*, will make the image less distinct again).

Because our pupils do not close completely, we often squint in bright light. By bringing our eyelids closer together we can further reduce the amount of light reaching the retina through the pupil (Fig. 46). Even so, our eyes are not well adapted to extremely bright light, and we ordinarily need sunglasses or some other artificial aid to reduce light if we are going to spend more than a few minutes in very bright sunshine.

By reducing spherical aberration, squinting also helps to make clearer some objects that would otherwise be less distinct. Again, choose some object that is too near or too far from your eye to be seen as clearly as you would wish to see it. Now, by bringing your eyelids so close that only a small slit remains between them, you should be able to see the object more distinctly.

Not only does squinting reduce the amount of light entering the eye, it also reduces the field of vision. Unlike the iris, which is immediately against the lens in most eyes, the eyelids are separated from the lens by some distance. Thus, when they come close together, they block *all* the rays of light from some objects before you. If only for this reason, squinting is not the most efficient way to reduce the amount of light reaching the retina. Neither is it a substitute for glasses should you need them.

One more thing about pupils that we should consider is shape; but first return once more to your magnifying glass, waxed paper, and cardboard. Select one of the holes that you have already made, and with the hole on the far side of the lens and up against it, focus a bright sunny scene on the waxed paper. Now move the cardboard so that the hole is in different positions: exact center of the lens, a little above center, to the right of center, and so on. You will notice that it makes no difference where the hole is: the same scene will be focused on the waxed paper. Figure 47 shows you why. You might also like to refer to Figures 12 and 40.

No matter where the light rays from any point on the object enter the lens, they come to focus at the same point on the waxed paper (once again, we ignore spherical aberration, which would be slight). If it doesn't matter where the hole in the cardboard is with reference to the lens, then it

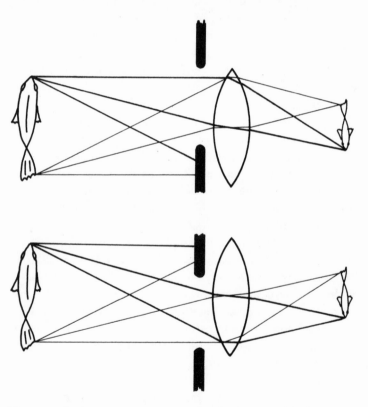

Fig. 47. It does not matter much which rays of light are blocked out before light reaches a lens. A similar image is formed no matter where the opening is.

shouldn't matter what shape the hole is either. Cut some holes of various shapes in the cardboard and try focusing with them one at a time. The images of the same scene should always look the same except for changes in brightness when two holes let in different amounts of light. Be sure, of course, that the cardboard is directly against the lens.

Not only does the shape of the hole not matter, the num-

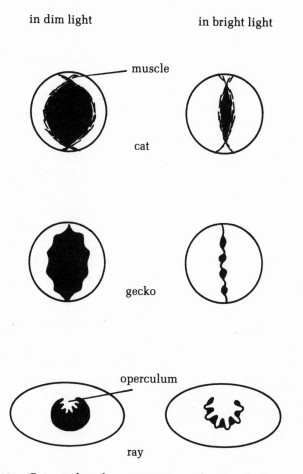

in dim light   in bright light

muscle

cat

gecko

operculum

ray

Fig. 48. *Cats and geckos are nocturnal animals that are active during at least part of the day. The ray is a deep-sea fish that sleeps at the surface of the ocean by day.*

ber of holes does not matter either. Cut two or more small holes close together and place them before the lens as you focus. Again, you should see the same scene on the waxed paper, and you will see it once, not several times. (But you will see several more or less indistinct images when they are *not* in focus.)

The *slit pupil* is one of the eye adaptations of some nocturnal animals that sleep in bright sunshine. Unlike round pupils, slit pupils can close either completely or nearly completely, thus protecting the eye more than the round pupil can. The iris with a slit pupil has the dilator and sphincter muscles that we have already described for the round pupil, but it has, in addition, two sets of muscle fibers that criss-cross above and below the pupil (Fig. 48). When these muscles contract, they close the pupil from side to side but not from top or bottom. The pupil thus becomes narrower and forms a vertical slit. When these muscles and the sphincter muscle relax, the pupil widens. In darkness, the pupil is perfectly round or nearly so. Among the animals with slit pupils are cats, chinchillas, crocodiles, and nocturnal snakes. In some frogs and toads the pupil does not close to a slit but only to a broad or narrow oval or even a diamond or heart shape.

One of the most unusual slit pupils is found in geckos, which are nocturnal lizards living primarily in tropical areas. The iris has a notched margin, and it has a complicated set of muscles. As the pupil closes, parts of the opposite edges overlap but leave four small openings between them.

In some animals the iris bears an extension called an *operculum*. It enlarges in bright light and shades the pupil (Fig. 48). The opercula of different animals have various shapes, and so the unshaded portion of the pupil also varies in shape.

CHAPTER 7 / Seeing More or Seeing Better

NOT ALL ANIMALS see the world in the same way, nor do they need to. Different animals lead different kinds of lives, and therefore they need different kinds of information about the world around them. Consider only two kinds of animal: herbivore and predator.

Herbivores are animals that eat plants, and they usually are the prey of predators, which are animals that eat other animals. Herbivores, therefore, need to know where their food plants are and where any nearby predators might be. In either case, it is usually more important for the herbivore to know the direction in which the plants or predators are, rather than their exact distance from him.

Think first of food. Because herbivores eat plants, their food does not run away from them. A horse does not have to pounce carefully on a tuft of grass for fear that it will run away. If he knows that there is grass growing near his feet, all he has to do is to keep lowering his head, and his mouth will hit the grass. Even if the grass is growing in tufts with a little bare ground between them, the horse need only move his head from side to side along the ground and he will run into some grass. A horse does not have to see his food at the moment his mouth reaches it. In fact, a horse—and many other herbivores—cannot see his food at the moment he takes it into his mouth, for a horse's eyes are so placed in its head that he cannot see what is near his face and directly before it.

When it comes to predators, it is important for a horse to know if a predator is too far away to be dangerous or close enough to have some possibility of catching him. But once the predator comes close, the horse runs away. It does not matter if the predator is ten feet or two feet behind him, the horse has been frightened and does his best to escape. What the horse needs to know is which direction to run; and this, of course, depends on where the predator is. Because a predator could approach from any direction, it would be advantageous for the horse to be able to see in every direction at once, and this is what many herbivores can do.

Herbivores typically have eyes on the sides of their head, each eye seeing approximately half of the landscape around the animal (Fig. 49). This type of vision is called monocular (which means "one-eyed"), because nearly everything the animal sees is seen by only one eye at a time. If the animal has bulging eyes—because of the curvature of the corneas, as with some nocturnal animals—each eye may be able to see through an angle of 180° or more. Depending on exactly how the eyes are positioned, the animals can see either a full circle around themselves or nearly a full circle. In Figure 50, the field of vision of each eye of two herbivores is indicated by single hatching. The area that both eyes see is indicated by crosshatching. In many herbivores there is

Fig. 49. *The pronghorn antelope, like most other herbivores, has its eyes on opposite sides of its head.*

very little overlapping of the fields of vision, and when the overlapping does occur it is usually to the front of the head —and possibly to the rear as well. Notice that when the eyes are on opposite sides of the head, there is a small area directly in front of the head (and also one behind) that the animal cannot see. This is why a horse cannot see what he eats at the moment he eats it. He can see something directly before him only if it is far enough away.

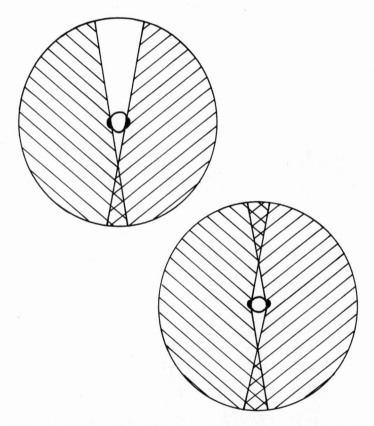

Fig. 50. Monocular vision. In most herbivores the fields of vision of the two eyes overlap to the front (above); in a few the two fields overlap both to the front and to the rear (below). Where the fields overlap, vision is binocular. Animals with monocular vision usually have an area immediately in front of the head where they cannot see.

The shape of the head or of the body behind may also determine how much the animal can see, for a large, bulky body can block the field of vision behind. Animals usually have some adaptation that permits them to look around their bodies, at least from time to time (Fig. 51).

With only one eye seeing an object, an animal has difficulty determining how far away that object is. You can test this for yourself by holding one long, newly sharpened pencil in each hand, the points facing each other but at least a

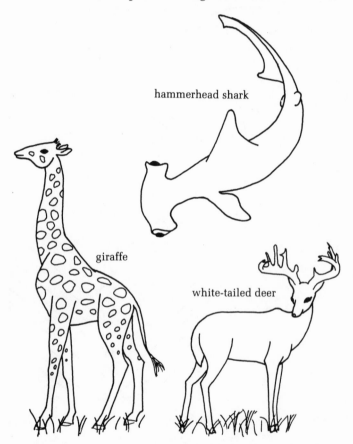

Fig. 51 *Animals with monocular vision have adaptations that allow them to see around their own bodies. The giraffe and the white-tailed deer have long necks, and the hammerhead shark has an unusually wide head.*

foot apart. Hold them near the eraser end (Fig. 52). Then, with one eye closed and the other open, try to bring the points together. Unless you are rather lucky, the two points will probably slide past each other without touching. If you try this repeatedly, you may eventually succeed, but the success then probably will be due to the fact that your arms finally got the "feel" of where the pencils were and not because your eye could tell if the points were going to touch.

If you try one more time to make the points touch, but this time do it with both eyes open, you will probably succeed immediately. This results from the fact that when two eyes attached to the same brain view the same object simultaneously, the brain can judge the distance to the object with some degree of accuracy. As both of your eyes watch the two pencil tips nearing each other, your brain can tell which one is a little closer to you, and a slight movement of your hand is all that is necessary to correct the movement of one or both pencils and prevent them from sliding past each other.

Animals that can judge distance accurately usually have both eyes placed in the front of the head, where the fields of vision of the two eyes overlap a great deal (Fig. 53). Such vision is called *binocular* ("two-eyed") vision; whatever object the animal concentrates on is seen by both eyes simultaneously.

Predatory animals typically possess binocular vision (Fig. 54). Predators feed on other animals, which are not likely to stand still and allow themselves to be eaten. When

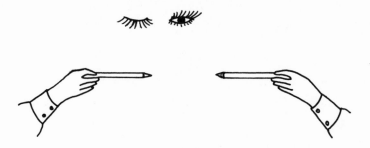

Fig. 52. *How to demonstrate that binocular vision is better than monocular vision in calculating distance.*

the prey animal flees, the predator must know not only in what direction the prey runs, but it must also be able to recognize when it has come close enough to take the final action—a swipe with the paw, a bite on the neck, a leap onto the back—that will bring the prey down. If the predator misses, even by only an inch or two, the prey may escape. Therefore, judging distances accurately is important to predators, as it is not to herbivores.

Other groups of animals for whom binocular vision is important are those that live in trees and jump from limb to limb: monkeys, apes, cats, and others. Not only must they see their intended destination clearly, they must be able to tell exactly how far away it is. Missing a branch by only an inch could mean serious injury or even death.

Animals that manipulate their food by using their front paws like hands also have binocular vision. These include monkeys, apes, and raccoons. Your experiment with the two pencils should make you understand the reason for this.

Binocular vision also makes it relatively easy to determine the three-dimensional shape of an object. Our ability to invent and to make new tools depends in part on our ability to see in three dimensions, and beyond that our ability to think about all three dimensions simultaneously.

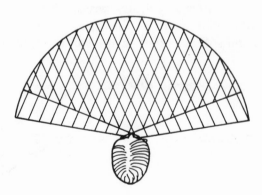

Fig. 53. *Human beings have binocular vision. The fields of vision of our two eyes are nearly the same, for the two eyes are placed in the front of the head and face forward.*

Without binocular vision, there probably would be no human civilization today.

Binocular vision does have the disadvantage of not allowing an animal to see behind its head. However, the larger, more ferocious predators are not likely to be attacked by others, and if a monkey's life depends on his seeing the

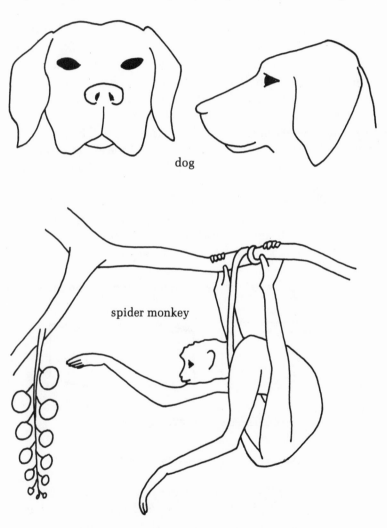

dog

spider monkey

Fig. 54. *Animals with binocular vision usually are predators, live in trees, or use their paws as hands.*

branch toward which he is swinging, there would not be much advantage in his being able to see the branch he just left. Many animals are agile enough to turn around or to turn their heads from time to time to see behind them. An owl can turn its head 270°, which has given rise to the belief that an owl can turn its head around a complete circle, which it cannot.

An animal with binocular vision is able to judge distances and shapes because the two eyes that look at the same object are some distance apart—the farther the better, but this, of course is limited by the size of the head. Each of the two eyes looks at an object from a slightly different angle, and therefore the retinas of the two eyes receive slightly different images of the same thing. Hold a small box or book about a foot from your face and look at it one eye at a time. It will look different to each eye. Hold the box so that your left eye barely sees the right side of the box and barely sees the top of the box. Now if you look at it one eye at a time— without moving it—you will notice that the sides and top seem to have different shapes as you switch from eye to eye (Fig. 55). This is because each eye sees it from a different position.

When you have both eyes open and focused on the box,

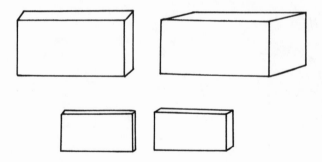

Fig. 55. *If we look at a box one eye at a time, the box appears different with each eye (left and right). The farther away the box, the less the apparent difference in the box (above and below). This difference, plus the difference in apparent size, helps us to judge the distance to the box.*

the optic nerves send to the brain information about the two different images of the box, but you see only a single box. Somehow, in ways no one fully understands, the brain takes information about two separate, different, flat images and fuses this into information about the three-dimensional shape of the box. Whatever the brain does, it is more than just superimposing one image on the other. If you use tracing paper to trace the two drawings of the box in the upper half of Figure 55 and then lay one tracing on the other, you will not have a three-dimensional drawing of the box. You will have a confusing set of lines that probably is less useful to you than either drawing alone. The brain does a much better job than that.

Not only does the brain's fusing of the information about the two images let you see the box in three dimensions, it also helps you to determine how far away the box is. Hold the box before your eyes again with the top and

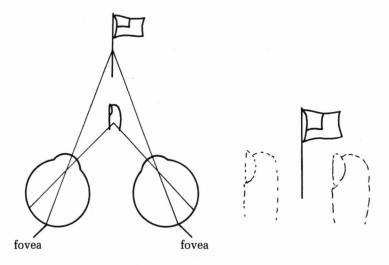

fovea   fovea

Fig. 56. *When both eyes focus on a distant flagpole, the two images of the flagpole fall on the foveae of both eyes. At the same time, the images of a finger fall on noncorresponding parts of the retinas. As a consequence we see one flagpole and two fingers.*

right side barely visible to your left eye, but this time keep it at arm's length. When you look at it with each eye separately, the sides will again seem to have different shapes, but the difference between them will not be as great as when the box was closer to the eye.

Now put the box on a table about five or six feet away from you and look at it again, one eye at a time. Again, what each eye sees will be different, but the difference will be even less. Repeat this at twenty or thirty feet, and there will not be much difference in what your two eyes see. Therefore, depending on how much alike or how different the two images are, the brain can judge the distance to the box. The more nearly alike the two images are, the farther away is the object.

We might pause here to mention that during our waking hours we see most things double, although we hardly ever notice it. To demonstrate this, select something rather far

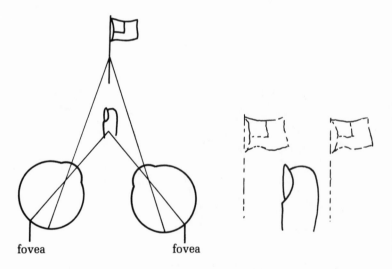

fovea   fovea

Fig. 57.   When both eyes focus on a near finger, the two images of the finger fall on the foveae, but the images of the flagpole fall on noncorresponding parts of the retinas. Then we see one finger and two flagpoles.

away from you—perhaps a flagpole down the street or a picture on the wall at the far side of a large room. While your eyes focus on the distant object, hold a finger up at arm's length. The finger should be on a direct line between your nose and the distant object. You should see one flagpole, but two fingers (Fig. 56).

We say that the eyes are *converging* on the distant flagpole. When the eyes converge on an object, the two images fall on corresponding parts (the foveae) of the retinas of the two eyes, and the brain can fuse the two images. Because the two eyes are not converged on the finger, the two images of the finger fall on parts of the two retinas that do not correspond, and the brain cannot fuse the two images, and so you see your finger twice. If you alternately open and close your two eyes, while still focusing on the flagpole, you will see that the right eye sees the "left" finger and the left eye sees the "right" finger.

Now focus both eyes on the finger; that is, make your eyes converge on the finger. You should see one finger and two flagpoles (Fig. 57). The images of the finger fall on the foveae, and the images of the flagpole fall on noncorresponding parts of the retinas. Now the right eye sees the "right" flagpole and the left eye sees the "left" flagpole.

Ordinarily, we do not notice these extra fingers or flagpoles in our field of vision for at least two reasons: (1) when we concentrate on one object, we do not pay much attention to others, and (2) these double objects are out of focus, and we tend not to notice what is out of focus.

When an object is at a distance of more than about twenty feet, the images on our two retinas are nearly the same; and beyond that distance, it becomes difficult to judge the exact distance by binocular vision. However, when we most need to judge distances accurately and quickly, we are usually concerned with something nearby. You cannot trip over a log that is twenty feet away; you need be concerned about how high to raise your feet only when the log is immediately before you. You cannot fall over a cliff that is twenty feet away, so you need be concerned about its exact location only after you come much closer to it. Because most of us cannot jump twenty feet, we have little difficulty judging the distance to the place we plan to land when we do jump.

This does not mean that there is no way for us to judge relative distances beyond twenty feet, or for a one-eyed person to judge distance at all. There are several clues that help us to estimate distances, though none is quite so accurate as binocular vision.

We are all familiar with the sizes of certain things, and we know that they appear larger when they are near, and smaller when they are farther away. A house that appears to us to be no taller than a nearby cat must be much farther away than the cat (Fig. 58). A bee that appears to be larger than the automobile parked across the street must be very close to your eye.

If one object blocks or partially blocks our view of another, then we know that the former is the closer.

Fig. 58. *We can judge relative distances if we are familiar with the sizes of objects. Because we know a cat is smaller than a house, we infer that this cat must be closer than the house.*

If you change your position in relation to two or more objects, you may be able to tell which is nearer. The position of the nearer object will appear to change faster than that of the more distant object. You have perhaps noticed this when you ride in an automobile (Fig. 59). Trees or telephone poles near the road seem almost to fly past you, but a mountain in the distance seems hardly to move at all.

Even tilting your head will sometimes enable you to tell which of two objects is nearer, or determine the distance of one object, because it puts your eyes in slightly different positions (Fig. 60). When an animal with monocular vision moves its head repeatedly back and forth, it may be getting the next best thing to binocular vision—putting one eye alternately in two positions. By viewing the same object from two positions in rapid succession, the animal probably can judge distance. For this reason, the long neck of a swan or a camel may be an advantage because it allows the animal to put its eye in positions that are far apart; and the farther apart the positions are, the better the distance can be judged. Some sharks and some other carnivorous fishes that have eyes placed rather more to the side of the head than we would expect for typical predators on land (Fig. 51), have the habit of circling their intended victims several times

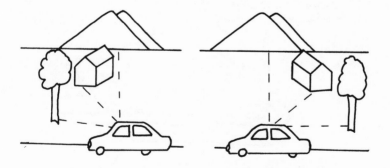

Fig. 59. *Another way to judge distance is to change your own position. The apparent position of a nearby object will change more rapidly than will the apparent position of distant objects.*

before striking. This puts the near eye in many different positions, relative to the victim, and so may enable the animal to judge striking distance.

However, we cannot always rely on what our eyes tell us about distance. Air contains some combination of dust, soil particles, soot, minute droplets of water, and other small particles. These tend to make the air look hazy, more some days than others, depending on the amount present. The greater the distance through which we look to see an object, the hazier the air will appear to be. Therefore, when looking

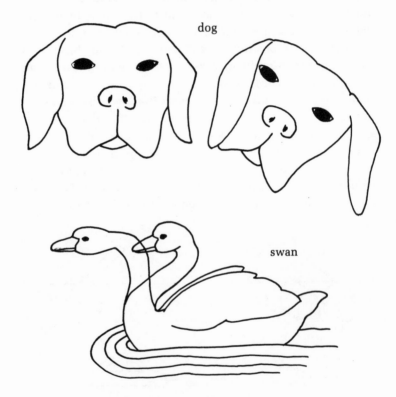

Fig. 60. *Animals with binocular vision may be able to judge distances of near objects merely by tilting the head and by putting the eyes in a slightly different position (above). Animals with monocular vision move their heads back and forth when estimating distance (below).*

across a landscape, we sometimes judge the distance of trees or mountains by how clear or hazy they look. But, in places where the air is unusually clear or unusually foggy or smoggy, we usually misjudge. In clear, dry, unpolluted air we tend to think that a distant mountain is much closer than it is. On the other hand, if we do manage to see a tree or house looming through a dense fog, we usually believe it to be farther away than it is.

Thus far in this chapter we have discussed only those animals that might be considered to be typical herbivorous animals and typical carnivorous predators. There are other animals that are omnivorous (eating both plant and animal material), and there are animals that, because of where they live or how they live, have eyes with some unusual features.

A robin, for example, is a predator—it eats earthworms. But it is also preyed upon by larger predators, such as cats or hawks. A robin's eyes are set on the sides of its head more like those of an animal preyed upon than like one that preys.

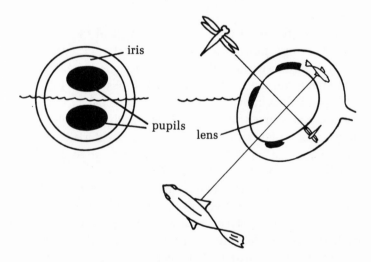

Fig. 61. *The four-eyed fish has only two eyes, but each eye has two pupils, one below the water line and one above. Different areas of the retina receive images from above and below the water line.*

When we see a robin hunting earthworms in a lawn, we are inclined to think that the tilting of his head means he is listening for worms. Rather, he is looking for worms with one eye and watching for danger with the other.

The squirrel is an herbivore and might become the victim of a cat or a hawk, yet it must judge distances as it runs from tree limb to tree limb. A squirrel's eyes are on the sides of its head, but they are tilted far enough forward and upward to give squirrel binocular vision to the front and also allow it to see above its head. Therefore, a squirrel running along the ground or on a horizontal branch can see a hawk above, and a squirrel running up or down a tree trunk can see a cat approaching from a branch. A squirrel's eyes are placed much like those of the rat in Figure 37.

One bird, the least bittern, can see under its head. This adaptation seems to be correlated with another one: the bird's ability to hide among reeds and grasses by "freezing" with its beak pointing straight upwards. The bird's markings make it nearly invisible among the grasses in this position, and its eyes can then see danger approaching from the front or sides.

One of the most unusual eyes is that of the four-eyed fish, *Anableps tetrophthalmus*. This fish of Central and South America swims at the surface and searches for insects both above and below the water line. It has, in reality, only two eyes, but each eye has two pupils, one below the water line and one above (Fig. 61). The lens is approximately egg-shaped, and each end, with its own characteristic curves, functions like a separate lens. The upper pupil and the narrow diameter of the lens focus light rays from above the water surface onto the lower part of the retina. The lower pupil and the long diameter of the lens focus light rays from below the water surface onto the upper part of the retina. Each eye, therefore, functions much as if it were two eyes forming images of different subjects.

CHAPTER 8 / *Insect Eyes*

THE EYES OF VERTEBRATES (animals with backbones)—with which we have been largely concerned in the last four chapters—are all rather similar. They have the same general structure, with only those variations that adapt the eyes to the particular life style of the animal. The eyes of invertebrates (animals without backbones) are of so many different kinds that a small book could not possibly discuss all of them. We have, so far, touched on the rather simple ocellus of *Dugesia* and the pinhole eye of *Nautilus*. In this chapter we will discuss the eyes of another group of invertebrates—the insects. Insect eyes are of two main types: compound eyes and simple eyes.

COMPOUND EYES

Most adult insects see through a pair of compound eyes (Fig. 62). A compound eye consists of usually hundreds or thousands of similar units called *ommatidia*. The ommatidia are packed closely together, and at the surface of the eye they form a hexagonal pattern.

Each ommatidium (which means "little eye") contains its own lens and photoreceptor, and so is like a very simple eye. However, the angle of view of each ommatidium is narrower than that of many other simple eyes—the ocellus of *Dugesia*, for example. Because each ommatidium of a compound eye looks out at the world from a different angle, each ommatidium sees something different. What the entire eye sees is a composite of what all the ommatidia see.

The way images are formed by the compound eye varies from species to species, but two main types of compound eye are: the apposition eye and the superposition eye. There are numerous variations on these two types, just as there are variations on the vertebrate eye.

The word *appose* means to place things side by side. In the *apposition eye* the ommatidia produce separate images that form side by side within the eye. Each individual image is of only a small part of the object being viewed; all these images together form one large image of the entire object.

In each ommatidium of an apposition eye, two structures focus light rays: a corneal lens and a crystalline cone (Fig. 63). The *corneal lens* is part of the insect's cuticle, a nonliving secretion that covers the entire insect. Over the eyes the cuticle is transparent, and the part over each ommatidium has the shape of a tiny lens. Under the corneal lens is the *crystalline cone*, which consists of living cells and functions as another small lens.

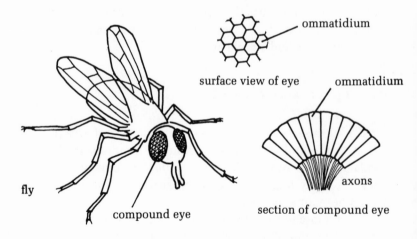

Fig. 62.   *Adult insects have two compound eyes with ommatidia arranged in a hexagonal pattern.*

Below the crystalline cone are several neurons called *retinula cells*—often six, seven, or eight in an ommatidium. All the retinula cells of all the ommatidia form the retina of the compound eye.

Axons of the retinula cells extend directly to the brain; there is no optic nerve as in our own eyes. At any one time, an ommatidium can send out only six, seven, or eight impulses—no more than it has retinula cells. Furthermore, because the axons of the retinula cells all converge on one neuron in the nervous pathway, the brain actually receives fewer impulses per ommatidium than might otherwise be the case. It is believed that in most insect eyes each ommatidium functions as a unit sending only one message to the brain at a time, but this is not certain.

Where the retinula cells meet in the center of an ommatidium they form a long, rod-shaped structure called a *rhabdom*. In an apposition eye, the rhabdom is directly beneath the crystalline cone and touches it.

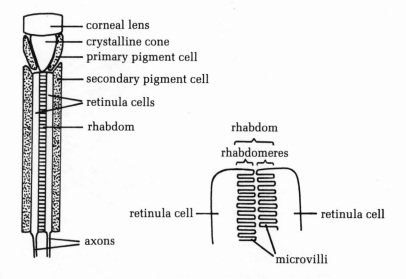

Fig. 63. *Section through the ommatidium of an apposition eye (left). Detail of a portion of two retinula cells to show the microvilli of which the rhabdom is composed (right).*

In most insects the rhabdom is formed by the meeting of extensions of the retinula cells. These extensions, called rhabdomeres, are believed to be the modified dendrites of the retinula cells. They are the photoreceptive portion of the ommatidium, and they correspond to the rods and cones of our rod cells and cone cells. Each rhabdomere consists of numerous fine tubular structures called microvilli, which are extensions of the surface of the retinula cell. They lie perpendicular to the long axis of the rhabdomere—just as

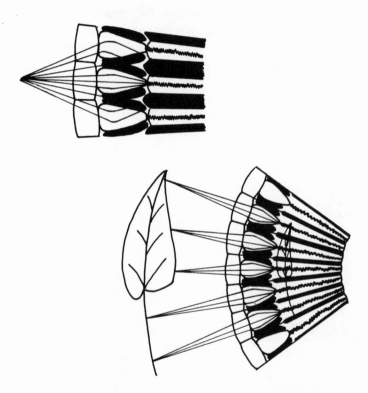

Fig. 64. Sections of an apposition eye. Light radiating from one point may enter several ommatidia, but light rays that are absorbed by pigment cells never reach a rhabdom (above). The image formed by a compound eye is not inverted like the images formed by a vertebrate eye with its single lens.

our thylakoids lie perpendicular to the long axis of our rods and cones (compare Figures 26 and 63).

The microvilli are believed to contain photoreceptive pigments. Insect eyes, like all other eyes that have been examined for pigments, contain rhodopsin. There is evidence that the eyes of those insects that can distinguish colors contain other pigments that are sensitive to light of only certain colors.

Surrounding the crystalline cone are several *primary pigment cells,* which contain a dark pigment that probably is melanin. Surrounding the set of retinula cells are several *secondary pigment cells.*

Light that enters the ommatidium by passing through the corneal lens parallel with or nearly parallel with the long axis of the ommatidium will be focused on the rhabdom (Fig. 64). Light that enters at a sharper angle will strike a pigment cell, which absorbs it. This prevents the light from passing into another ommatidium, and so it never reaches a rhabdom. In an apposition eye, then, each rhabdom receives only the light that passes through the corneal lens and crystalline cone of its ommatidium. Each ommatidium forms a separate image on its rhabdom. All the ommatidia together form a large, mosaic image.

Apposition eyes are characteristic of diurnal insects, which are active by day, when the light is bright. Because the pigment cells absorb so much light that the insects never see, these eyes might be described as "wasteful" of light. But the absorption of light by the pigment cells keeps each ommatidium seeing only what is directly before it, and this makes the vision of the apposition eye acute. It may also protect the visual pigments, which might be destroyed if all the light of a bright day were to reach the rhabdoms.

Acuity of an insect eye also depends on the number of ommatidia in an eye and on the size of the ommatidia. This refers not to their length but to the area in the field of vision each ommatidium covers. Of course, the smaller the field of view each ommatidium covers, the smaller the ommatidia themselves are likely to be, and the more ommatidia there can be in an eye of a given size. The most acute insect eyes are large apposition eyes with many small ommatidia (Fig. 65).

As with vertebrates, the position of an insect's eyes correlates with its way of life. (Fig. 66). Herbivorous insects, especially those that do not fly or jump, have little need for binocular vision, and their eyes usually are positioned on the sides of their heads where they can see predators approaching from all or nearly all directions. Like herbivorous vertebrates, they have only a very narrow field of binocular vision.

Predatory insects and those that fly or jump do have need to judge distances, for they must be able to judge accurately the distance to prey or a landing spot. Such insects have eyes that can see forward, and this gives binocular vision. But even the predatory insects are small, especially when compared with other animals, and are likely to be

Fig. 65. *A compound eye with a few large ommatidia forms a coarse image, but an eye with many small ommatidia forms an image with more detail. Compare with Figure 29.*

eaten by some predator larger than they. So, unless they have some other protection from predators, they too, need to see all around them, and their eyes usually can see to the side and to the rear as well. Some can also see above and below them. For example, the praying mantis, which is one of the larger, predatory insects, and the dragonfly, which is an expert flier, have large, bulging eyes that give them a "bug-eyed" look. These eyes can see in virtually all directions except back into the head. Of course, the ommatidia that look out to the side provide only monocular vision.

Our own judgment of distance depends to a great extent on our ability to converge both of our eyes on the same object (Chapter 7). Most insects cannot move their eyes and so cannot converge them, but an insect with binocular vision has

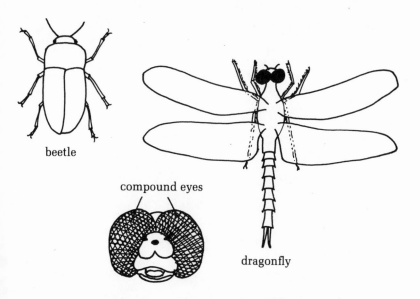

beetle

compound eyes

dragonfly

Fig. 66. *Herbivorous insects usually have eyes that point to the side and provide monocular vision (above left). Predatory insects and insects that are strong fliers usually have large compound eyes that provide binocular vision toward the front and perhaps also above and below; in addition they have monocular vision to the sides (right and below).*

another way of determining distance. This method depends on the fact that each ommatidium looks out in a slightly different direction, and that at least some ommatidia from the two eyes see the same thing simultaneously.

If, for example, the two ommatidia indicated by single hatching in Figure 67 see an object at the same time, that object is at a certain distance, because this is the only distance at which it could be viewed simultaneously by these two ommatidia. If the two ommatidia indicated by crosshatching see the object at the same time, then it must be closer, for this is the only distance at which it could be viewed simultaneously by these two ommatidia. Therefore, depending on which ommatidia see something together, the insect can judge distance.

In fact, the insect can determine not only distance, but direction, by the same method. When either of the two pairs

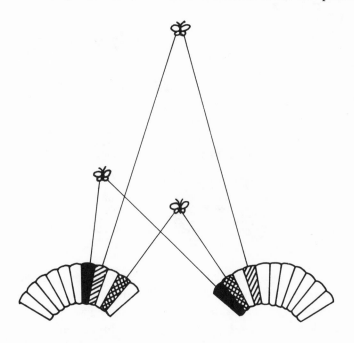

Fig. 67. *Insects with binocular vision can judge distance and location of an object by which ommatidia see it simultaneously. See text for more information.*

of ommatidia we just mentioned see an object simultaneously, that object is directly in front of the insect. When the object is seen simultaneously by the two ommatidia indicated in black, then the object is off to one side. If the object attracts the insect's attention, then the insect probably will turn toward it, thus bringing it into the center of its field of binocular vision.

Of course, the insect does not consciously know the exact distance between itself and other things in its environment. Rather, when the insect's brain receives nervous impulses from a certain combination of ommatidia, the brain automatically sends to other parts of the body nervous impulses that cause them to bite, to jump, to turn, or to do whatever is appropriate under the circumstances, and to do it to the proper distance.

The second main type of compound insect eye is the *superposition* eye. The word *superpose* means to place one thing on top of another. In the superposition eye, images formed by several ommatidia are superposed one on the other instead of forming side by side as in the apposition eye. Superposition eyes are characteristic of nocturnal insects.

An ommatidium of a superposition eye differs from one in an apposition eye in two important ways. The rhabdom does not touch the crystalline cone but is separated from it by some distance; only a narrow filament, an extension of the retinula cells, connects the rhabdom and crystalline cone (Fig. 68). Furthermore, the dark pigment in the secondary pigment cells is confined almost entirely to the ends of those cells around the crystalline cone. Therefore, between the crystalline cone and the rhabdom of a superposition eye, there is a clear, transparent zone occupied by the clear portions of the secondary pigment cells and the filaments of the retinula cells. With no dark pigment separating ommatidia in the clear zone, light entering an ommatidium from an angle and then refracted sharply by the corneal lens and the crystalline cone, may pass through one, two, or more ommatidia before reaching a rhabdom. In the superposition eye several rays of light radiating from one point on an object and reaching several different ommatidia are all brought back into focus on one rhabdom. Or, to put it another way, several images of that point are superposed on one rhabdom.

In some superposition eyes, as many as thirty images

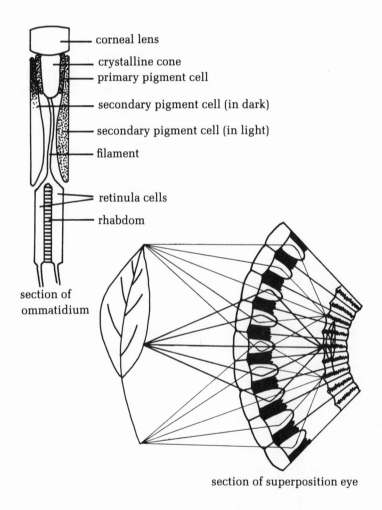

corneal lens

crystalline cone
primary pigment cell

secondary pigment cell (in dark)

secondary pigment cell (in light)

filament

retinula cells

rhabdom

section of
ommatidium

section of superposition eye

Fig. 68.   Superposition eye. Light reaching several
ommatidia can be focused on a single rhabdom if the
pigment in the secondary pigment cells is in the upper part
of the cells, as it is at night.

from thirty different ommatidia may form one superposed image on one rhabdom. This makes the image much brighter than one formed by an apposition eye—provided both eyes are viewing an object at the same, low light intensity. This makes the superposition eye much better for seeing at night than the apposition eye, for it makes much more efficient use of light. However, the superposition of many images does make the images less distinct. As among vertebrates, insect eyes adapted to night vision are more sensitive to light but have poorer acuity than eyes adapted to vision in bright light.

Some nocturnal insects have a tapetum lucidum at the base of the retinula cells. This functions like the tapetum lucidum of cats and many other nocturnal vertebrates; any light that passes once through the retinula cells without being absorbed may be absorbed by them when it passes back after being reflected by the tapetum. The tapetum of the insect eye is made of small branching tubules that are part of the respiratory system.

Many superposition eyes can adapt to bright light merely by the redistribution of pigment throughout the entire secondary pigment cells. This forms a dark barrier between ommatidia for about half their length, and this is sufficient to prevent light rays from passing from ommatidium to ommatidium after they leave the crystalline cone. Therefore, in bright light, the superposition eye may function much like an apposition eye (Fig. 68).

In some insects, different parts of the eye have different types of ommatidia. In the praying mantis, for instance, the forward part of the eye, which is involved in binocular vision, has ommatidia of the apposition type, and other parts have ommatidia of the superposition type.

It is important to note that in any compound eye, although the corneal lens and the crystalline cone in each ommatidium can form a good, clear image of whatever lies in its field of vision, the image falls on only one rhabdom. Therefore, only one—or perhaps a few—nervous impulses may be sent to the brain from each ommatidium, and the brain "sees" this merely as a dot of light. The brain perceives

an entire object as a series of dots of light or darkness because each ommatidium views a different part of the object.

Whether the image is an apposition one or a superposition one, it is an erect one, and not an inverted image like
the one the single lens in our own eye makes. Because the
entire image is formed by many small lenses, each produc-
ing its own tiny image, the individual images are in the same
order as the ommatidia that formed them.

The insect eye has no means of adjusting its focus as our
eyes do. This, too, is related to the structure of the compound eye. Because each ommatidium sends to the brain
information about only a single "dot" of light, it does not
matter much whether that small image is in sharp focus or
not when it hits the rhabdom. What does matter is whether
or not light does strike a rhabdom, and if it does, which
rhabdom receives it.

SIMPLE EYES

In addition to compound eyes, many adult insects have two
or three simple eyes called *dorsal ocelli*, and the larvae and
pupae of some insects have simple eyes called *stemmata*, or
lateral ocelli (Fig. 69). Dorsal ocelli usually are located between the two compound eyes. Stemmata are on the sides of
the head. The number of stemmata varies according to species of insect, from few to many.

In most dorsal ocelli there is a single lens formed by a
thickening of the cuticle, and below it are several retinula
cells with rhabdoms (Fig. 70). Because the image formed by
the lens does not fall on the rhabdoms, it seems unlikely that
insects can perceive form with their dorsal ocelli. Furthermore, the number of rhabdoms in most dorsal ocelli is too
small to produce a detailed image even if the rhabdoms were
in the plane of focus.

Dorsal ocelli seem to be involved in perception of light
intensity, and the lens probably concentrates light in the
general area of the photoreceptive cells rather than focusing
it with precision. In some insects this perception of light

intensity is important in maintaining a daily activity rhythm. Nervous messages are probably sent from the dorsal ocelli to the brain that it is now light (at sunrise) or that it is now dark (at sunset). Some insects are attracted to light, others normally move away from it; if the dorsal ocelli of either kind of insect are covered with black paint, the insects no longer respond in the way they normally do. This is

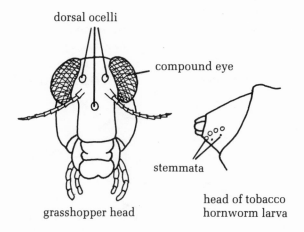

dorsal ocelli

compound eye

stemmata

grasshopper head

head of tobacco hornworm larva

Fig. 69. *Head of an adult grasshopper showing dorsal ocelli (left). Head of a hornworm caterpillar showing stemmata of two sizes (right).*

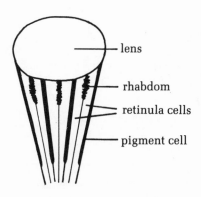

lens

rhabdom

retinula cells

pigment cell

Fig. 70. *Section of a dorsal ocellus.*

strong evidence that in these insects perception of light intensity by dorsal ocelli is involved in movement toward or away from light.

The dorsal ocelli of some nocturnal insects have a tapetum lucidum.

The structures of stemmata vary a great deal. Some are rather like dorsal ocelli, with a lens and a retina of several to many rhabdoms—thousands, in some insects. On the other hand, a stemma with only a few retinula cells may have only one rhabdom (Fig. 71). In mosquito larvae, the stemmata are little more than a few photoreceptors surrounded by darkly pigmented cells; these are sometimes called *pigment spots*.

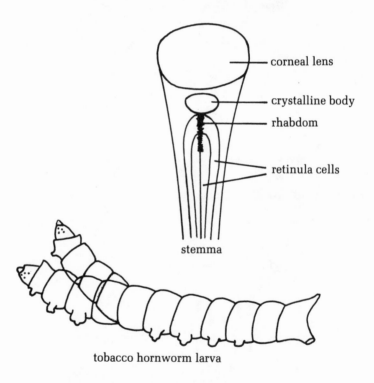

corneal lens

crystalline body

rhabdom

retinula cells

stemma

tobacco hornworm larva

Fig. 71. *Section of a stemma (above). Hornworm larvae moving head, which probably allows it to perceive form although the individual stemmata cannot.*

There is no lens, but the photoreceptors are sensitive to light, and the larvae respond to it.

Most stemmata—if not all—cannot produce an image detailed enough to show form. This is either because: (1) no image forms at all because there is no lens; (2) there is only one or a few rhabdoms, and this is not enough to produce a clear image; or (3) the image produced by the lens falls behind the retina. Nonetheless, many stemmata do seem to be involved in the perception of form. As the insect moves its head back and forth, even one stemma with only a single rhabdom can perceive changes in light and dark as the head's position changes in relationship to the object being viewed. If there are several stemmata, then some or all of them may be gathering similar information from just slightly different positions at the same time.

This is a little like a blind person determining the shape of an object by moving his fingers over it. He cannot have his fingers everywhere on the object at once. But if he runs only one finger over it, his brain will remember what he felt at each moment, and when he is finished, his brain will have gathered together all this information, and he will know the shape of the object. If he uses all his fingers at once, he can determine the shape more quickly and more efficiently.

If a caterpillar with a half dozen stemmata on one side of its head moves its head back and forth, its brain will remember what each stemma saw (just a spot of light or darkness) at each moment and put all the information together. In this way, the brain will "know" the shape of an object, even though each individual stemma saw very little at any one time.

In all likelihood, the insect's impression of an object viewed through one stemma or a group of stemmata is a rather coarse, indistinct one, but undoubtedly it is good enough to cause the insect to approach or flee, depending on what the object is.

CHAPTER 9 / *Seeing with Mirrors*

A LENS IS NOT the only device that can focus an image. A curved mirror can do it, and so can a set of many small, flat mirrors. All the eyes with lenses that have appeared so far in this book are refracting eyes—their lenses bend light rays as the light passes through them. This chapter will be concerned with *reflecting eyes*—eyes that reflect rays of light from a tissue that acts like a mirror. The tissue may be arranged as one curved surface in the form of a parabola, or it may consist of many small, flat mirrors within the ommatidia of a superposition eye.

EYES WITH PARABOLIC MIRRORS

If it is to focus an image on the retina of an eye, a single mirror must be of the correct shape. A single flat mirror will focus nothing on a retina. Take, for example, your flat bathroom mirror. When light rays from your body strike your bathroom mirror, they are reflected back from the mirror (Fig. 72). Imagine that a line perpendicular to the surface of the mirror is drawn so that it touches the mirror exactly where a ray of light from your body meets the mirror. The angle formed between the perpendicular line and the light ray traveling to the mirror is called the *angle of incidence;* the angle formed between the perpendicular line and the light ray leaving the mirror is the *angle of reflection.* The angle of incidence and the angle of reflection are always equal. Because these angles are equal and because you see only the reflected rays, you see what appears to be yourself standing behind the mirror. Of course, no one is there. Only the image of yourself is there, and that image really doesn't exist. The light rays from your body have not passed through the mirror or through the place where your image seems to

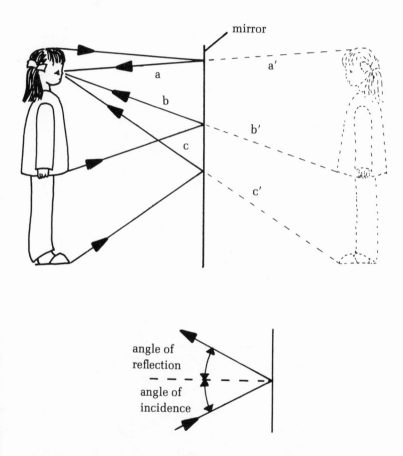

Fig. 72. *Virtual image seen in a mirror. Rays a, b, and c give the impression of a virtual image on the far side of the mirror. Ray a looks as if it began as a'. Ray b looks as if it began as b'. Ray c looks as if it began as c'. Yet a', b', and c' do not exist.*

be. This kind of image is called a *virtual image*. It is not a real one; a virtual image merely appears to be where it is not.

All the images we have discussed in earlier chapters have been *real images*. Real images are formed by the actual meeting of light rays in space. A real image exists where it appears to be.

For an eye to really see an object, a real image must be focused on the retina. In an eye with a lens that forms the image, the retina must be behind the lens, for that is where the real image forms; but in an eye with a single mirror

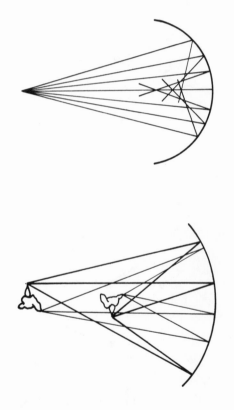

Fig. 73. *A hemispherical mirror brings light rays to such a poor focus that no good image is formed (above).*
A parabolic mirror forms an inverted image (below).

focusing the image, the retina must be in front of the mirror, because that is where the real image forms.

Now to the shape of the mirror in an eye. This mirror could not be flat, for no real image would be formed on the retina. However, a curved mirror of proper shape will focus an image (Fig. 73). This will not be a mirror shaped like a perfect hemispherical bowl though, because such a mirror will produce such a poorly focused image as to be practically worthless. The best shape for a focusing mirror is a *parabola*. A parabola is a type of curve that never closes on itself as a circle or an oval does. A parabolic mirror forms a real image of an object on the concave side of the mirror.

A lens is not absolutely necessary with a parabolic mirror, but if there is no lens only the central area of the image the mirror forms is distinct. The outer part of the image is somewhat deformed. To correct this, a lens must be placed so that the light passes through the lens before it reaches the mirror. The lens refracts the light rays slightly, and this alters slightly the angle at which they meet the mirror. Because the angle of reflection equals the angle of incidence, the angle of the reflected ray is also changed. If the lens is of the proper shape, the entire image that results is distinct. The eyes of a scallop focus light this way—with a parabolic mirror and a corrective lens. The image forms between the lens and the mirror.

Scallops are shellfish that live in a shell composed of two valves—like clams and oysters. The living portion of the scallop has about fifty small eyes, which are visible only when the valves of the shell open. Each eye is backed by a thick, dark, pigmented tissue. To the front of this is the curved mirror, which consists of a thin layer of living, reflective tissue (Fig. 74). Then come two layers of retinal cells, and then the lens. At the very front is the cornea. The mirror is approximately parabolic in shape, and it focuses light on the retina. Any light not absorbed by the retina continues out of the eye. If you look directly into a scallop eye you can see the shiny mirror surface within it.

Two things about the scallop lens are unusual. One is its shape; its forward surface bulges a great deal at the center, then becomes slightly concave near the edge. And another is the fact that the lens touches the retina; there is no space between the lens and retina as in our own eyes. Both of these unusual features are related to the fact that the lens does not focus light on the retina. It merely refracts the light rays slightly as they enter the eye. Because the lens does not focus light on the retina; there is no need for a space between it and the retina.

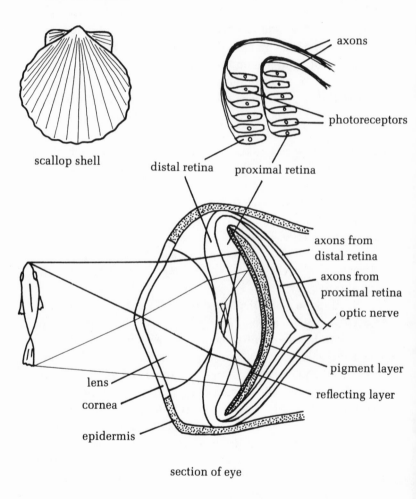

Fig. 74. *The scallop eye. See text for details. The parabolic reflecting tissue is indicated by cross hatching.*

The scallop eye has two layers of photoreceptive cells in the retina. The layer closer to the rear of the eye (also closer to the mirror) is the *proximal retina*. The layer farther from the mirror is the *distal retina*. The mirror focuses light on the distal retina. The photoreceptors of the distal retina are activated when light goes off rather than when it goes on. The distal retina probably functions as a motion detector that warns the animal of the movement of possible enemies nearby.

The photoreceptors of the proximal retina, which does not receive a sharp image, are activated when light goes on. It is believed that the proximal retina can detect large areas of light or darkness in the environment. The animal then moves toward the light or darkness—whichever is appropriate at the moment.

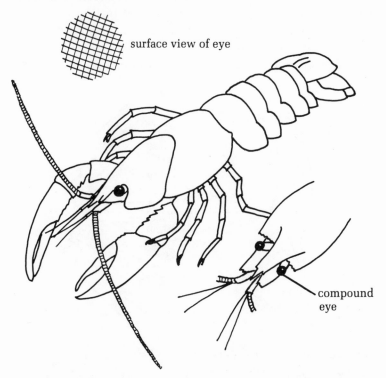

surface view of eye

compound eye

Fig. 75.   *The crayfish has two compound eyes on movable stalks. The ommatidia are arranged in a square pattern.*

The axons from the distal and proximal retina form separate branches of the optic nerve. Although the branches unite and form one common optic nerve, the axons from the two retinas have no communication with each other but merely run side by side.

COMPOUND EYES WITH MIRRORS

Crayfish (Fig. 75), lobsters, and shrimp belong to a group of animals called macruran crustaceans. Crustaceans are related to insects, and like insects they have compound eyes. Most crustacean eyes have ommatidia that focus with a corneal lens and a crystalline cone as the insect ommatidia do. However, in the eyes of macruran crustaceans, the lens and crystalline cone do not have sufficient refracting power to focus light on the rhabdoms. Most of the focusing is done by hundreds or thousands of tiny, flat mirrors.

The macruran eye is a superposition eye. In general

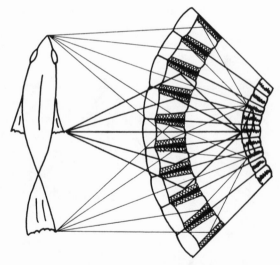

Fig. 76. Section of the eye of a crayfish, which functions like the superposition eye of an insect, but light is reflected by mirrors rather than being refracted by lenses. The reflecting tissues are indicated by crosshatching.

structure it resembles the superposition eye of nocturnal insects (Fig. 76). There is a clear space between the crystalline cones and the rhabdoms, and dark pigment lies between the crystalline cones but does not extend down into the clear zone. Therefore, as in the insect superposition eye, light entering the eye through one ommatidium can pass to the rhabdom of another.

But the macruran eye, unlike the insect eye, has ommatidia that are square in cross section; the pattern on the surface of the eye is like a checkerboard rather than a honeycomb of hexagonal cells. And the upper part of the inner surface of the four walls of each ommatidia are lined with reflecting surfaces—miniature mirrors.

Light rays radiating from one point on an object being viewed by a crayfish enter several adjacent ommatidia and are reflected by their mirrors onto the rhabdom of one ommatidium. Thus, as in the nocturnal insect eye, several images of a single point are superposed on a rhabdom. As in the insect eye, the total image on the retina is an erect one. Being a superposition image, it is also a bright one.

No single mirror focuses light, and all the mirrors are flat. But, as in the insect eye, it does not matter whether the light striking a rhabdom is in sharp focus or not; for whatever light reaches the rhabdom is perceived by the brain as a dot of light. The entire array of many small mirrors, each in a position slightly different from its neighbors, reflects light onto several rhabdoms. In this sense the entire array may be said to focus an image on the retina.

More About Eyes

This book is not really finished. There is much more that could be written about eyes. For those who want to read further, the following books and articles may be interesting. You might also try browsing in your library among the books devoted to particular animals. If, for instance, you are particularly interested in eyes of spiders or birds, then check the books on spiders or birds. Some of them, especially the larger, more comprehensive books, may have a chapter or part of a chapter devoted to eyes. In addition, most encyclopedias have articles on eyes and vision.

BOOKS

Bullock, Theodore Holmes, and G. Adrian Horridge. *Structure and Function in the Nervous Systems of Invertebrates*, 2 volumes. San Francisco: W. H. Freeman & Co., 1965. This is a very large work that describes the nervous systems of all groups of invertebrates including their eyes. College level.

Clayton, Roderick K. *Light and Living Matter*, Volume 2: *The Biological Part*. New York: McGraw-Hill Book Company, 1971. This is a paperback book devoted to ways that light affects living things. One chapter is concerned with vision in higher animals. Includes material on the chemical changes in rhodopsin when light strikes the retina. College level.

Gregg, James R. *Experiments in Visual Science For Home and School.* New York: Ronald Press, 1966. This is a collection of simple experiments that can be performed quite easily, although a few require equipment that most persons would not have at home.

Mueller, Conrad G., Mae Rudolph and the Editors of *Life. Light and Vision.* New York: Time Incorporated, 1966. This book covers the vision of animals in general.

Noback, Charles R., and Robert J. Demarest. *The Human Nervous System: Basic Principles of Neurobiology.* New York: McGraw-Hill, 1975. This book covers the entire human nervous system. One chapter is devoted to the eye and vision. Good description of the retina.

Walls, Gordon Lynn. *The Vertebrate Eye and Its Adaptive Radiation.* Bloomfield Hills, Mich.: The Cranbrook Press, 1942. Although this book is quite old, it has a lot of good material on the eyes of all groups of vertebrates. There is, of course, no modern material about the retina.

ARTICLES

Anonymous. "Eyeing Animals Eyeball to Eyeball." *Smithsonian*, February, 1971. This very short article is illustrated with twenty beautiful color photographs by Constance Warner. They include a photograph of scallop eyes with their mirrors clearly shining as they reflect light back out of the eyes.

Horridge, G. Adrian. "The Compound Eye of Insects," *Scientific American*, July, 1977.

Kennedy, Donald. "Inhibition in Visual Systems." *Scientific American*, July, 1963. This article is concerned with inhibition in vision in several invertebrate animals.

Land, Michael F. "Animal Eyes with Mirror Optics." *Scientific American*, December, 1978.

Michael, Charles R. "Retinal Processing of Visual Images." *Scientific American*, May, 1969.

Ratliff, Floyd. "Contour and Contrast." *Scientific American*, June, 1972.

Wald, George. "Eye and Camera." *Scientific American*, August, 1950.

Werblin, Frank S. "The Control of Sensitivity in the Retina." *Scientific American*, January, 1973.

White, Harvey E., and Levatin, Paul. " 'Floaters' in the Eye." *Scientific American*, June, 1962. This article presents a possible explanation for those hazy spots we all occasionally see floating in our field of vision.

Glossary

accommodation: changing of focus of the eye

acuity: keenness or sharpness of vision

amacrine cell: a type of retinal neuron that improves detection of movement

angle of incidence: the angle between a line perpendicular to a surface and a ray of light striking that surface at the same point

angle of reflection: the angle between a line perpendicular to a surface and a reflected ray of light leaving the surface from the same point

apposition eye: a compound eye in which the image formed by each ommatidium is projected onto its own rhabdom; apposition eyes are characteristic of diurnal insects

aqueous humor: fluid in the front chamber of the eye

arrhythmic animals: animals that are active by both day and night

axon: that portion of a neuron that conducts impulses away from the cell body and toward another neuron

binocular vision: vision characteristic of animals with eyes to the front of the head; the fields of vision of the two eyes overlap a great deal

bipolar cell: a type of retinal neuron that transmits impulses from photoreceptors to ganglion cells

blind spot: the portion of the retina at which the axons of ganglion cells pass into the optic nerve; because there are no photoreceptors in this area, we cannot see any image that falls on it

cell body: the portion of a neuron that contains the nucleus

choroid: the middle layer of the wall of the eye; the choroid contains blood vessels

ciliary body: a muscular tissue in the eye from which the lens is suspended by suspensory ligaments; the contraction and relaxation of the ciliary muscles controls the focusing of the lens

concave lens: a lens that is thicker near the edge than in the center; such a lens corrects myopia (nearsightedness)

cone: the light-sensitive dendrite of a cone cell

cone cell: one of the two types of photoreceptor in the retina; cone cells are involved in color vision

converge: to meet at a point, as when the axons of several neurons converge on the dendrite of another; also to have both eyes aimed at the same object

convex lens: a lens that is thicker in the center than at the edge; such a lens corrects hypermetropia, a type of nearsightedness

compound eye: an eye composed of many small repeating units called ommatidia; compound eyes are characteristic of insects and some related animals, including crayfish and other crustaceans

cornea: the transparent portion of the sclera at the front of the eye; the cornea, together with the lens, focuses light on the retina

corneal lens: a lens formed from the cuticle over a compound eye

crepuscular animals: animals that are active at dusk

crystalline cone: a lens formed of living cells in a compound eye

dendrite: that portion of a neuron that either receives or initiates a nervous impulse and conducts it toward the cell body

dilator muscle: a muscle, which when it contracts, enlarges an opening as with the pupil of the eye

distal: farthest from the body or point of attachment

diurnal animals: animals that are active by day

farsightedness: a condition of having difficulty seeing nearby objects; presbyopia and hypermetropia are two types of farsightedness

fovea: the portion of the retina that has only cone cells; each cone cell has its own ganglion cell that carries impulses to the brain; the fovea is the area of most acute vision

ganglion cell: a type of retinal neuron that transmits impulses from bipolar cells to the brain; axons of ganglion cells form the optic nerve

herbivore: an animal that eats plants

horizontal cell: a type of retinal neuron that improves detection of contrast

hypermetropia: a type of farsightedness caused by having eyeballs shorter than normal; a person with hypermetropia has difficulty seeing nearby objects

inferior oblique: one of the muscles that rotate the eyeball

inferior rectus: the muscle that moves the eyeball down

invisible light: light of wavelengths shorter than 380 nanometers or longer than 760 nanometers; we cannot see anything by this light alone; invisible light includes ultraviolet and infrared

iris: the colored tissue that surrounds the pupil and controls its size

lateral rectus: the muscle that moves the eyeball away from the midline of the head

lens: a piece of transparent material so shaped that it focuses light rays

medial rectus: the muscle that moves the eyeball toward the midline of the head

melanin: a black or dark brown pigment found in several parts of the body; in eyes, it is in those tissues that prevent some rays of light from reaching the photoreceptors, as, for example in the pigment epithelium and iris of our eyes or the pigment cup of the ocellus of *Dugesia*

microvillus: a very fine tubular extension from the retinula cells of insect eyes

monocular vision: vision characteristic of animals with eyes on the sides of their head; the fields of vision of the two eyes overlap very little

myopia: nearsightedness; a condition of having difficulty with distance vision because of having eyeballs longer than normal

nanometer: a billionth of a meter

nearsightedness: a condition in which there is difficulty with distance vision because of having eyeballs longer than normal; myopia

neuron: a nerve cell; neurons transmit nervous impulses

nocturnal animals: animals that are active at night

ocellus: the simple eye of many invertebrates

ommatidium: one of the small, repeating units that form a compound eye; each ommatidium is a "little eye"

optic nerve: a nerve consisting of the axons of ganglion cells that extend from the retina to the brain

parabola: a type of bowl-shaped curve; a parabolic curve never closes on itself

photoreceptor: a cell, which, when stimulated by light, sends a nervous impulse toward the brain

pigment epithelium: a layer of dark, pigment-containing cells at the rear of the retina

pinhole eye: the eye of *Nautilus*, which focuses by means of a pinhole

plasma membrane: the membrane that surrounds the living portion of a cell

predator: an animal that eats other animals

presbyopia: a type of farsightedness caused by the inability of the lens to change shape; this condition often develops in middle age

primary pigment cells: pigment-containing cells that prevent passage of light from ommatidium to ommatidium at the level of the crystalline cones in a compound eye

proximal: nearest to the body or point of attachment

pupil: the opening in the iris

real image: an image formed by the intersection of light rays in space

refraction: the bending of light rays as they pass from one transparent substance to another

retina: the inner, light-sensitive layer of the wall of the eye; the retina contains the photoreceptors

retinula cells: photoreceptor cells in the simple and compound eyes of many invertebrates

retinula club: the light-sensitive portion of the retinula cells of *Dugesia*

rhabdom: the light-sensitive, rod-shaped structure in the ommatidia of insect eyes; it consists of the rhabdomeres of all the retinula cells in the ommatidium

rhabdomere: the light-sensitive portion of a retinula cell in the ommatidium of an insect eye; it consists of many microvilli containing visual pigments

rhodopsin: the visual pigment in rods; also called visual purple

rod: the light-sensitive dendrite of a rod cell

rod cell: one of the two types of photoreceptor in the retina; rod cells are not involved in color vision

sclera: the outer layer of the wall of the eye

secondary pigment cells: one of the pigment-containing cells in the ommatidium of compound eyes; these cells prevent passage of light from one ommatidium to another in apposition eyes and, in bright light, in superposition eyes as well

spherical aberration: the failure of a lens or mirror to bring all the light rays emanating from a single point into focus

sphincter muscle: a circular muscle, which, when it contracts, closes an opening as with the pupil of the eye

stemma: one of the simple eyes at the side of the head of some insect larvae and pupae

superior oblique: one of the muscles that rotates the eyeball

superior rectus: the muscle that moves the eyeball up

superposition eye: a compound eye in which images formed by several ommatidia are projected onto the rhabdom of one ommatidium; superposition eyes are characteristic of nocturnal insects

suspensory ligaments: fibers that hold the lens in place and change its shape as the ciliary muscles contract or relax

tapetum lucidum: a reflecting tissue behind the retina of some nocturnal animals

thylakoid: a flat, membranous disk in some cells; in photoreceptors, thylakoid membranes contain the visual pigments

virtual image: an image formed by light rays that appear to intersect in space but actually do not

visible light: light of wavelengths of 380 to 760 nanometers; this is the light we see things by

visual pigment: a photoreceptor pigment, which, when struck by light, causes the initiation of a nervous impulse in the photoreceptor

visual purple: rhodopsin; the visual pigment in rods

vitreous: jellylike substance in the rear chamber of the eye

Index

amacrine cell, 33, 45, 48, 50
Anableps tetrophthalmus
  (four-eyed fish), 82
angle of incidence, 98-99
angle of reflection, 98-99
apposition eye, 84-91
aqueous humor, 23
arrhythmic animals, 59-66
axons, 35-36

bending of light rays
  See: reflection, refraction
bipolar cell, 33, 47, 48, 50
blind spot, 44-45

cell body, 35-36
cell membrane (plasma
  membrane), 36-37
choroid, 22
ciliary body, 22, 27-28
ciliary muscles, 27-28
color vision, 39-40
compound eye
  of crayfish, 104-105
  of insects, 83-94
concave lens, 29
cone, 36-42, 52, 58, 60
cone cell, 23, 33, 36, 50
contrast detection, 47-48
convex lens, 29

cornea, 22, 23
corneal lens, 84, 91
corrective lens (of scallop
  eye), 101
crayfish, 104-105
crepuscular animals, 59
crystalline cone, 84, 91, 105

dendrite, 35-36
dilator muscle, 54
distal retina (of scallop eye),
  103-104
distances, judging, 70-72,
  76-81, 89-90
diurnal animals, 58-59, 84-91
dorsal ocellus, 94-96
Dugesia (Planaria), 8-11, 15

eyes of
  arrhythmic animals, 59-66
  cats, 57, 66
  crayfish, 104-105
  crepuscular animals, 59
  diurnal animals, 58-59, 84-91
  Dugesia (Planaria), 8-11, 15
  fish, 26
  four-eyed fish, 82
  gecko, 66
  herbivores, 67-70, 88
  human beings, 22-50

insects, 83-97
macruran crustaceans,
104-105
Nautilus, 11-15
nocturnal animals, 50-57, 66,
91-94
predators, 71-72, 88-89
scallops, 101-104
eyeshine, 57

farsightedness, 29
flatworm (Dugesia), 8-11
focusing
with a lens
with a magnifying glass,
19-21, 24, 54-56, 63-66
with lens of a fish eye, 26
with lens of a human eye,
23-28
with mirrors
in compound eye of
crayfish, 104-105
parabolic mirror of scallop
eye, 98-104
with a pinhole
in cardboard, 12-15
in a Nautilus eye, 11-15
four-eyed fish, 82
fovea (fovea centralis) 39-42,
77

ganglion cell, 33, 40, 48, 50
gecko eye, 66

horizontal cell, 33, 45, 47, 50
human eye, 22-50
hypermetropia, 29

incidence, angle of, 98-99
inferior oblique muscle, 32
inferior rectus muscle, 31
invisible light, 7
iris, 22, 54, 66

judging distance, 70-72, 76-81,
89-90

judging shapes, 72-76, 97

lateral ocelli
See: stemmata
lateral rectus muscle, 31
lenses, 16-21
concave, 29
convex, 29
corrective lens of scallop
eye, 101
of diurnal animals, 59
of fish eyes, 26
of human eyes, 23-29
light, 3-7
invisible, 7
reflection of, 98-99
refraction of, 16-21
visible, 6-7
wavelengths of, 5-7

macruran crustaceans, 104-105
medial rectus muscle, 31
melanin, 33, 87
microvilli, 86
mirror, parabolic, 101
monocular vision, 68-70
movement detection, 48-49
Muller's cell, 50
muscles of eyeball, 31-32
See also: ciliary muscles
myopia, 29

nanometer, 5
Nautilus, 11-15
nearsightedness, 29
neurons, 35-36
nocturnal animals, 50-57

ocelli
of Dugesia, 8-11, 15
of insects
dorsal ocelli, 94-96
pigment spots, 96
stemmata (lateral ocelli),
96-97

ommatidia, 83-94, 104-105
operculum, 66
optic nerve
    of human eye, 33
    of Nautilus, 11
    of scallop eye, 104

parabolic mirror, 101
photoreceptors, 3, 33, 35, 41,
    47, 50
    See also: cone cells, retinula
    cells, rod cells
pigment cells (of Dugesia), 8
pigment cup (of Dugesia), 8-10
pigment epithelium, 33-35, 60
pigment spots, 96
pinhole, 11-15
    comparison with lenses,
        20-21
    pinhole eye of Nautilus,
        11-15
plasma membrane, 36
predators, 71-82
presbyopia, 29
primary pigment cell, 87
proximal retina (of scallop
    eye), 103-104
pupils
    of arrhythmic animals, 62-66
    of four-eyed fish, 82
    of nocturnal animals, 53-56

rainbow colors, 6
real image, 100
reflecting eyes, 98-105
reflection, 98-99
reflection, angle of 98-99
refraction, 16-21, 23
retina
    of human eye, 22-23, 33-50

of Nautilus, 11
of scallop eye, 103-104
retinula cells
    of Dugesia, 8-11
    of insects, 85, 91
retinula clubs, 9
rhabdom, 85, 91-92, 94, 96-97,
    105
rhabdomere, 86
rhodopsin, 37
rod, 36-37, 39-43, 52, 59, 60
rod cell, 23, 33, 36, 50

scallop eye, 101-104
sclera, 22
secondary pigment cell
    in apposition eye, 87
    in superposition eye, 91, 93
shapes, judging, 72-76, 97
slit pupils, 66
spherical aberration, 62-63
sphincter muscle, 54
stemmata, 96-97
superior oblique muscle, 32
superior rectus muscle, 31
superposition eye
    of crayfish, 104-105
    of insects, 91-94
suspensory ligaments, 27

tapetum lucidum, 56-57, 93
thylakoids, 36-37

virtual image, 100
visible light, 6-7
visual pigments, 3, 5, 37
visual purple (rhodopsin), 37
vitreous, 23

wavelengths of light, 5-7